THE STONE CIRCLES OF CUMBRIA

The
STONE CIRCLES
of CUMBRIA

John Waterhouse

Phillimore

1985

Published by
PHILLIMORE & CO. LTD.
Shopwyke Hall, Chichester, Sussex

© John Waterhouse, 1985

ISBN 0 85033 566 3

Printed and bound in Great Britain by
THE CAMELOT PRESS
Southampton, England

To Liz, Helen and Stephen

> ... remnants huge
> Of stone, or marble swart, their import gone,
> Their wisdom long since fled.

John Keats, *Hyperion*

Contents

List of Plates

(between pages 76 and 77)

List of Text Figures

Preface

Megaliths hold a powerful fascination for many people, quite apart from archaeologists and those concerned with prehistory. Every year many thousands of people visit the great stone circle of Castlerigg, near Keswick; but fewer manage to see the much larger circle of Long Meg and her Daughters, 20 miles away; and very few are aware that there are up to fifty stone circles, many difficult to find, located in and around the Cumbrian Fells. Few of the circles have been excavated, and much remains to be learned about them. For the visitor, all the sites, from the vast Long Meg circle to the diminutive circle on Bleaberry Haws near Coniston, have one great attraction in common: the sense of mystery associated with them, heightened by the wide panorama of the ever-present fells, the frequent glimpses of the Irish Sea and the solitude that is usually to be found in these ancient places.

This work attempts to present all that is known about these sites. It is the end result of many years of walking in Cumbria, during which I have gained an intimate knowledge of the sites and the countryside in which they lie. I owe a great debt to Aubrey Burl and his book *The Stone Circles of the British Isles*. This authoritative and well-written book inspired me to further study, and convinced me of the worth of writing a fuller account of this important group of stone circles. Many of the Cumbrian stone circles have been given different names by different authors, and where appropriate I have given preference to the names used by Burl.

I have divided the book into two main sections. Chapters One and Two form an introductory section: Chapter One summarises what is known of the prehistory of Cumbria up to the end of the early bronze age, and Chapter Two discusses current ideas on stone circles in general – their various types, shapes, and possible purposes and ages. Those readers who are not particularly interested in the technicalities of Chapters One and Two can happily concentrate on the major section – Chapters Three and Four. These two chapters form a detailed gazetteer of stone circles in Cumbria, both extant and destroyed; and this section is written to be used as a comprehensive guide to the sites. Many of the circles are easily visited, being close to roads; however, some are only reached after fairly strenuous walks, and full details of how to find these are given. Although there is free access to most of the sites, some of the circles are on private farmland, and permission to visit these must be obtained.

I hope that readers will experience some of the great pleasure that I have had since a child in walking in the magnificent countryside of the Lake District to visit these prehistoric sites.

Cambridge
Spring 1985

JOHN WATERHOUSE

Foreword

by *Dr. Jane M. Renfrew*, F.S.A, F.L.S.
Fellow of Lucy Cavendish College, Cambridge

The stone circles of the Lake District are amongst the most evocative prehistoric monuments in Britain. A visit to Long Meg and her Daughters inspired Wordsworth to write:

> 'A weight of awe not easy to be borne
> Fell suddenly upon my spirit, cast
> From the dread bosom of the unknown past,
> When first I saw that sisterhood forelorn; –
> And Her, whose strength and stature seemed to scorn
> The power of years – pre-eminent, and placed
> Apart, to overlook the circle vast.
> Speak Giant-mother! tell it to the Morn,
> While she dispels the cumbrous shades of night;
> Let the Moon hear, emerging from a cloud,
> When, how and wherefore, rose on British ground
> That wondrous Monument, whose mystic round
> Forth shadows, some have deemed, to mortal sight
> The inviolable God that tames the proud.'

The concentration of these monuments in this mountainous countryside is quite exceptional. John Waterhouse has visited, surveyed and collected detailed information about 50 stone circles in this area, and brought them together in this first systematic survey of these monuments. It is possible that they include some of the earliest stone circles in Britain, dating back to the neolithic, and that in this region they went on being constructed for more than 1,500 years. There is a great range of types – from the vast, monumental circles at Long Meg, Castlerigg and Swinside, to the standard early bronze age circles (approximately 100 ft in diameter) as at Casterton and Elva Plain, to diminutive rings associated with alignments and burials as at Lacra and Moor Divock. Some are of concentric form as at Oddendale and Birkrigg, or they may contain more than one burial cairn as at Burnmoor above Eskdale, or they may be associated with henge monuments as at Mayburgh.

John Waterhouse has spent many years visiting, recording and collecting information about these sights, and it is a great tribute to his dedication and tenacity that this project now comes to be published. Every year thousands of visitors pour into the Lake District – many of them may visit Castlerigg, above Keswick, but few will have known of the wealth of other stone circles tucked amongst the fells. To visitors and to specialists alike I commend this book and the circles it describes, and as one who began a similar survey many years ago, and gave up, I salute and congratulate the author on his successful completion of this fascinating study.

JANE M. RENFREW

Cambridge
March 1985

Acknowledgements

I would like to thank the following for permission to reproduce figures; detailed sources are given in the references.

W. Pennington-Tutin (fig. 1.1); K. Plint (fig. 1.2); C. Fell (figs. 3.9 and 3.26b); T. H. McK. Clough (figs. 1.3 and 1.4a, b, c); W. Fletcher (fig. 3.16); F. Barnes (fig. 3.26a); Cumberland and Westmorland Antiquarian and Archaeological Society (figs. 1.4e, 3.4, 3.20, 3.26c and d, 4.1, 4.2, 4.3, 4.4, 4.6, 4.7, 4.8, 4.13, 4.16, 4.17, 4.22, 4.23, 4.24); Oxford University Press (figs. 2.3 and 2.4); *Science* (fig. 2.5a); *Mathematical Gazette* (fig. 2.5b); Yale University Press (fig. 2.7); Royal Commission on Historical Monuments (England) (fig. 4.12).

The maps in figs. 3.5, 3.10, 3.24, 4.5, 4.10, 4.14 are based on Ordnance Survey maps, as also are the small 1:50,000 scale maps showing the site locations. Permission to reproduce these maps is acknowledged.

I have received advice and help from a number of archaeologists in the preparation of this book. I would like to thank Prof. Glyn Daniel, Prof. Colin Renfrew, Dr. Ruth Whitehouse and Dr. Roy Switsur for reading the text and for their comments and assistance. Any faults in the book, however, are mine alone. Special thanks are due to Dr. Jane Renfrew for her encouragement and help and for writing the Foreword.

I must express my deep gratitude to my colleague, Tony Carter, for drawing the maps and many of the figures, to my father, Sidney Waterhouse, for drawing the plans of the circles, and to David Starr for taking the cover photograph. Grateful mention must also be made of my two friends, Nick Williams and Rob Bryant, who on a number of occasions spent several days with me out on the hills surveying stone circles. Nick introduced me to the art of surveying. Without his great help and enthusiasm at the start of the project, it is unlikely that the work would have proceeded further.

My wife, Liz, has shown great tolerance and understanding during my absences in Cumbria and while I spent a good deal of my spare time in preparing the book. She has on many occasions acted as my unofficial literary adviser. To her go my heartfelt thanks.

Notes

i) *Plans of the Circles*
Unless otherwise acknowledged, the plans of the stone circles in this book have been drawn from surveys carried out by the author. The profiles of the stones are as seen from the centres of the circles.

ii) *Dating*
In this book actual (calendrical) dates are given as years 'BC', and radiocarbon (carbon-14) dates as years 'bc'.* Radiocarbon dates can be converted into dates BC from calibration tables, which have been compiled from measurements of radiocarbon dates of individual tree rings of certain long-lived species. These dates are then compared with the actual dates of the rings as determined by dendrochronology. The bristlecone pine of southern California has been of particular value for this purpose; but a new chronology, based on sub-fossil oaks from Irish peat bogs, has recently been published.[1] It is found that for times before 2,000 years ago, radiocarbon dates become increasingly too young as the ages of the samples increase (however, by about 8000bc the two sets of dates are approximately the same again). For a date of 5000bc the discrepancy is about 1,000 years. Several calibration tables have been published. Even so, the correction of radiocarbon dates is not without its uncertainties, and there is as yet no internationally accepted table, although there should soon be one. Recalibrated radiocarbon dates in this book are based on a table by Klein.[2] It should be pointed out that where a radiocarbon date is quoted with limits, e.g. 1800±100bc, there is only a 67 per cent chance of the actual date's being within the limits. Dates bc can be approximately converted to dates BC, or vice versa, by using the chronology chart in fig. 1.5.

*The term 'bc' is used here to represent radiocarbon dates rather than the convention term 'BP' in the hope that the dates will be more readily appreciated by the non-specialist reader.

Chapter One

Prehistoric Background

a) From Earliest Times to the End of the Early Neolithic Age (to c.2500bc, 3200BC)
There is no evidence for man's presence in Cumbria before the end of the last
glaciation, some 12,000 years ago. If man lived in this corner of Europe before this
time, ice and erosion have removed all trace of his occupation. The earliest
indication of human activity in Cumbria comes from Kirkhead Cave near
Grange-over-Sands, on the northern shore of Morecambe Bay. At some time after the
ice had retreated, upper palaeolithic hunters occupied the cave, perhaps using it as a
summer camp, and they left their flint tools there.[1]

Sites of mesolithic age have been discovered on the west Cumbrian coast. The
main locations are at the south end of Walney Island,[2] among the sand-dunes at
Drigg,[3] and in the vicinity of St Bees.[4] Microlithic flint tools of mesolithic type have
been found at these sites; and at St Bees implements of volcanic tuff were also
discovered, indicating that even at this early date man was utilizing igneous rocks
from the Cumbrian Fells. It is likely that the coastal area would have provided a
reasonable habitat for mesolithic man. The sandy areas were free from the
continuous forest cover of the hinterland; the sea was a source of food, often in the
form of shellfish; and the sea also provided the raw material for tool-making, in the
flint pebbles that are washed up on the beaches. Chalk, the rock in which flint
naturally occurs, is absent from Cumbria; and the flint found on Cumbrian beaches
is thought to be from a submarine outcrop of flint-bearing chalk in the Irish Sea.
'Caches' of flint pebbles, suggesting that they had been deliberately collected, were
found at Drigg, but in an undatable context.

Flint implements of later, neolithic, type have also been discovered on the
Cumbrian coast in similar locations to the supposedly mesolithic material. At North
End, on Walney Island, many neolithic flint implements and sherds of neolithic
pottery have been found on raised beach deposits.[2] Flint artifacts similar to these
have also been found at Drigg[3] and Eskmeals.[5] At the latter site, just to the south of
Drigg across the estuary of the Esk, flint implements, some of early neolithic type,
were discovered at several locations near the coast.

The close proximity of the mesolithic and neolithic artifacts suggests continuity of
activity at these sites. In fact, the sites may have been used for an even longer period
than the above finds indicate, as implements of early bronze age date were also found
at Eskmeals[5a] and Drigg.[3] Also at Drigg the remains of a timber structure and hearth
have been discovered in association with flint implements.[5b] A radiocarbon date
averaging at 2007bc was obtained from the site, indicating that it was in use at the
very beginning of the early bronze age. These coastal sites, however, provide little
evidence of permanent settlement in neolithic times, nor is it possible to date the

1

sites from the flint implements themselves. But when did neolithic settlers reach Cumbria? In order to answer this, evidence from other sources needs to be considered.

Neolithic people led an entirely different way of life from their hunter-gatherer predecessors of mesolithic times. As far as is known, neolithic people lived in settled communities and supported themselves largely by farming, both agricultural and pastoral. In order to do this they had to modify the environment that they encountered: they had to make inroads into the ubiquitous forest and cut down trees to provide clearings for their settlements, grazing-land for their cattle and fields in which to grow their crops. Their effect on the vegetational history of an area was at times profound and, in some cases, permanent. However, it is this effect on vegetation that helps us to answer the question of when these early farmers began their activities.

A very valuable technique for obtaining information on former vegetation is pollen analysis or 'palynology'. A 'rain' of pollen falls from plants; each species produces pollen grains of distinctive type which are identifiable by microscopic examination. Most of the pollen does not survive; but where the 'rain' falls in favoured locations the individual grains can be preserved. Pollen is best preserved in anaerobic and acidic conditions, such as those found in accumulating sediment at the bottom of shallow lakes and in growing peat bogs. A vertical column of sediment or peat therefore presents a record of the composition of the pollen 'rain' of a particular locality, and by inference a record of the local vegetational history. Such records often extend back over several millennia. Winifred Pennington has written an excellent review on the subject.[6]

One of the most significant horizons that occurs in the post-glacial records of many north-western European sites is known as the 'elm decline'. It is marked by a dramatic fall in the percentage of pollen from elm trees. Radiocarbon dates for the event have been obtained from many sites, and a date of 3200-3000bc (c. 3900BC) is consistently found. The elm decline is sometimes marked by changes in other tree pollen, but sometimes other trees seem little affected. Attempts have been made to account for the demise of the elm by changing climatic conditions; however, there is no convincing evidence for climatic change in the British Isles at this time.[6] There is also no direct evidence for a natural catastrophe such as Dutch elm disease, but this possibility cannot be ruled out. An explanation that has attracted much attention is that the elm decline was caused by early neolithic settlers. In support of this the date of the elm decline corresponds to dates obtained from the earliest neolithic sites by radiocarbon dating. The idea is due mainly to the Danish botanist Troels-Smith.[7] He envisages early neolithic settlers as pastoralists. In a forest-covered land with no natural grassland for grazing, the forest had to provide fodder; and a good source of fodder would have been elm leaves, which are particularly nutritious. The branches of elms were therefore selectively cropped, and hence the diminution in elm pollen alone. A suitable tool for this job would have been the polished stone axes of the early neolithic people. Firm evidence for early agriculture is provided by the presence of cereal pollen in the pollen profile; but such evidence is rarer than that for the initial exploitation of the forest as recorded in the elm decline. In Cumbria a few sites have yielded cereal pollen at a level somewhat above, and therefore later than, the elm decline.

The results of pollen analyses from some of the many Cumbrian sites that have been studied will show that, although the extent of human activity within Cumbria in early neolithic times was variable, an overall pattern emerges.

Barfield Tarn, on the coastal plain of west Cumbria near Bootle, has produced a radiocarbon date of 3390±120bc from a level just below that of the elm decline.[8] The elm decline here is marked by an initial drop in elm pollen only, with corresponding increases in the pollen of ribwort plantain and other weeds such as dock. These weeds are typical of pasture land. The elm pollen recovered somewhat before a second, marked, decline set in, and this also included a general decline in other tree species. At the time of the second decline the first appearance of cereal pollen occurs, and pollen from bracken and Compositae (the daisy family) increases sharply. These plants indicate a more open, grassy environment. The interpretation is that the initial drop in elm pollen indicates the use of elm leaves for fodder by pastoralists, who would also make small clearings in the forest for their cattle and their settlements. The sharper decline indicates a more vigorous attack on the forest; much larger areas were cleared for agricultural use. The dating evidence from this site indicates that early farmers began their activities on the west Cumbrian coast around the middle of the 4th millenium bc (c. 4000BC), in agreement with an earlier suggestion by Walker.[9] The pollen diagram from Barfield Tarn shows that the second clearance was progressive: the woodland never regenerated, and a vegetation of bracken and grasses remained predominant.[6] Together with similar evidence from other sites on the west Cumbrian coastal plain, this suggests that the coastal plain was largely deforested in the early neolithic period and has remained so ever since.

Evidence for two similar stages of land-use have been obtained from other sites in west Cumbria, including Ehenside Tarn[9] and the flint-working sites at Drigg[3] and

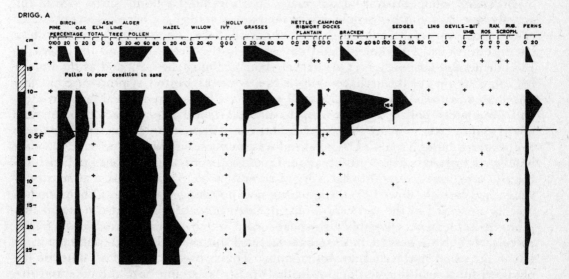

Fig. 1.1   A pollen diagram from Drigg. A struck flint flake was found at level S.F., after Pennington.[3]

Eskmeals.[6] At the Drigg site a flint flake was found *in situ* in a layer of peat just below the point where there was evidence for increased forest exploitation (a drop in tree pollen with an accompanying sharp increase in pollen from grasses and bracken). This is one of the few Cumbrian sites with a definite indication of human presence just before exploitation of the forest occurred (fig. 1.1).

Away from the western coastal region the sequence of early neolithic activity seems to have been somewhat different. From Urswick Tarn in south Furness, Oldfield found the expected two stages of land-use: an elm decline with no increase in weed pollen, followed by a general tree decline accompanied by an increase in the pollen of plantain and grasses.[10] Subsequently, however, the forest recovered to something like its former level. The inference is that the clearings were only temporary, and that the early neolithic settlers here practised a sort of 'shifting' agriculture, in contrast to the more settled pattern in the west. This may indicate a lower population in the Morecambe Bay area than on the western coastal plain.

Moving to higher land within the Cumbrian Fells, a slightly different picture appears. Pennington's work at Blea Tarn,[11] 150 m above sea-level near Great Langdale, has revealed two episodes of clearance, but they seem to be separated by a longer period of time than at the coastal sites. The elm decline is dated here at 3300-3200bc and probably resulted from the use of elm for fodder. The second episode of clearance, however, occurred through the 3rd millennium bc with a peak around 2500bc (*c.* 3200BC), perhaps associated with activity at the nearby axe factory site in Great Langdale.

Clearance of forest in the north of Cumbria, and by implication the onset of neolithic settlement, appears to have begun comparatively late. Pollen analyses from sites in the Carlisle lowlands and the north Eden valley reveal that settlement did not become widespread here until perhaps a thousand years after the first clearances on the west coast.[9]

Although pollen analyses from many localities in Cumbria show significant activity by early neolithic people, few of their settlements have been discovered. One of the most important ones is that of Ehenside Tarn. The site is 3 km (2 miles) south-south-west of Egremont, mid-way between the river Ehen and the coast. In 1869 the tenant farmer, John Quayle, set about draining the tarn; and as the waters fell away the first of the archaeological riches were discovered. A proper excavation was started in 1871,[12] and a considerable number of finds were made. Many partially and completely polished stone axes from the Great Langdale factory site were recovered; in fact, so many that 'shoemakers came from far and near and took them to sharpen their knives on'. One axehead was found mounted in its pierced wooden handle – a fortunate act of preservation. Proof that stone axes had been polished on the site was provided by the discovery of several pieces of sandstone and gritstone, which had been hollowed by the grinding and polishing processes. Other wooden objects preserved in the wet conditions included parts of a dug-out canoe and two pronged implements, possibly fish-spears. Also found was a quern, showing that cereals were grown here. A radiocarbon date of 3014±300bc has been obtained from one of the wooden objects that were found.[13] This is one of the earliest dates so far obtained for a neolithic settlement in the British Isles; and both the date and the implication for the use of cereals is in good agreement with the evidence from the pollen analysis at the same site.[9]

The radiocarbon date from Ehenside Tarn is one of the few dates that have been obtained from sites where polished stone axes from the Great Langdale factory site have been discovered. Polished stone axes have been considered the archetypal early neolithic implement. Their effectiveness at clearing woodland has been demonstrated by practical experiment;[14] but their initial use, if the above interpretation of the elm decline is correct, may have been in the cutting of the elm branches for fodder. In the chalkland areas of England flint was extensively used for axe-making, and mines were excavated to obtain the best quality flint from well below the surface. In the north and west of the country, where flint is not naturally occurring, neolithic man utilized types of igneous and metamorphic rocks that had similar flaking characteristics to flint, i.e. breaking with a conchoidal fracture. Several sources of rock used in axe-making are known, including sites in Cornwall, Wales and Cumbria.

The Cumbrian-type stone axe is characterized by its long slender shape, with roughly parallel sides and oval cross-section (fig. 1.2). The rock used in their manufacture is officially described as 'epidotized tuff of intermediate or basic composition belonging to the Borrowdale Volcanic series'.[15] Cumbrian axes composed of this rock are classified as Type VI. A smaller number of Cumbrian stone axes (Type XI) are made from a very similar rock.[13] Type VI axes have been found throughout Cumbria and at other sites in the British Isles; but it was not until 1947 that the location of the 'factory site' was discovered.[16, 17]

The factory is on the steep, south-west-facing scree slopes of Pike o'Stickle in the Langdale Pikes. The term 'factory', implying mass production of work, certainly seems apposite; for great concentrations of waste flakes, produced during the initial chipping stage of rough-outs, still lie on the scree slopes. Large numbers of roughed-out axes have also been found here: some broken, some rejected because of imperfections, and some seemingly well made. The final stage in the preparation of axes was the grinding and polishing of the rough-outs. No polished axes have been found at the factory site, and it is presumed that the finishing work was carried out at the settlement sites near the coast. Evidence for the grinding and polishing of axes at Ehenside Tarn has already been mentioned; and several other possible finishing sites have been found, such as Kell Bank near Gosforth,[18] and Stone Close, Stainton-in-Furness,[19] where rough-outs and grinding and polishing stones were discovered.

Excavation of a chipping site less than 1 km (½ mile) north of Pike o'Stickle has produced charcoal dated at 2734±135bc and 2524±52bc.[20] It may be that activity started at the Langdale site earlier than this, perhaps around the beginning of the 3rd millenium bc (c. 3800BC), as suggested by the early date from Ehenside and by pollen analysis from nearby Blea Tarn (p. 4).

Since the discovery of the Great Langdale site other, smaller, factory sites have been located in the fells: on the east flank of Scafell Pike, below the summit of Glaramara, at Spout Head, and on Seathwaite Fell[21] (fig. 1.2). One can only admire the ability of the early neolithic settlers to penetrate the central area of the Cumbrian Fells and locate the narrow outcrops of the ideal rock.

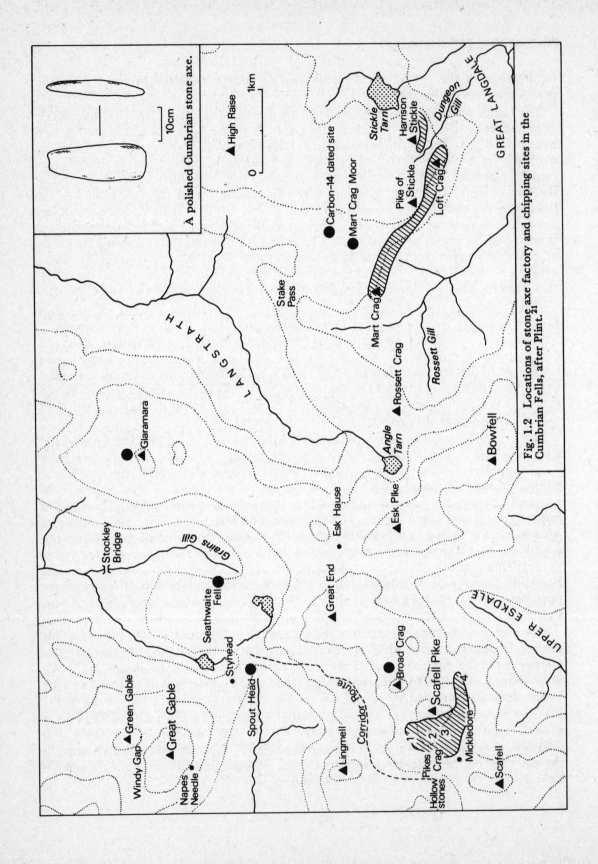

Fig. 1.2 Locations of stone axe factory and chipping sites in the Cumbrian Fells, after Plint.[21]

A polished Cumbrian stone axe.

10cm

0 1km

▲ High Raise

● Carbon-14 dated site
▲ Mart Crag Moor

Stickle Tarn

Harrison
▲ Stickle

Pike of
Stickle ▲

Loft Crag ▲

Dungeon Gill

GREAT LANGDALE

Mart Crag ▲

▲ Rossett Crag

Rossett Gill

Stake Pass

L A N G S T R A T H

▲ Glaramara ●

Angle Tarn

Esk Pike ▲

▲ Bowfell

Stockley Bridge

Grains Gill

Seathwaite Fell ●

Esk Hause ●

Great End ▲

Styhead ●

Spout Head ●

Windy Gap ●
▲ Green Gable

▲ Great Gable

Napes Needle ●

Corridor Route

Broad Crag ●
▲

Scafell Pike ▲

Lingmell ▲

Pikes Crag
Hollow Stones

1 2 3 4

Mickledore ●

▲ Scafell

UPPER ESKDALE

From the factory sites the roughed-out axes were transported to settlements throughout Cumbria. The possible routes followed have been traced from the isolated finds of flakes and rough-outs.[21, 22] It is interesting to note that many of the routes through the fells were along tracks still familiar to the fell-walker today (fig. 2.8). The trade-routes through Cumbria are discussed further in Chapter 2 in connection with the locations and dating of the early stone circles.

Trade in Cumbrian stone axes did not stop at the Cumbrian settlements; they have been found in many places in the British Isles, indicating that trade was conducted over long distances. Type VI axes have been found in southern England,[13] Lincolnshire,[23] and north-east England.[22] Cumbrian axes found in County Antrim[24] and the Isle of Man[17] show that sea-travel was used, and this form of transport may have been used to supply Cumbrian axes to southern Scotland.[17, 25]

There are few field monuments in Cumbria that can definitely be dated to the early neolithic period. Typical monuments of the period in other parts of the country are causewayed enclosures, long barrows, and megalithic chambered tombs. No causewayed enclosures are known in Cumbria, nor any proven chambered tomb. There are, however, some eight or 10 long barrows, more properly described as long cairns.[26, 27] Most are in the Eden valley area, such as the long cairn at Crosby Garrett (near Crosby Ravensworth) in which, in the 19th century, Canon Greenwell found several burials. Near the west coast are two further long cairns: Samson's Bratful, among the many smaller cairns on Stockdale Moor, and the possible long cairn on Skelmore Heads, just to the south of Ulverston.[29]

It is possible that the first of the great stone circles was raised in Cumbria at a late stage in the early neolithic period, some time during the last half of the 4th millenium BC.

b) Later Neolithic and Early Bronze Age (2500-1300bc, 3200-1600BC)
This is the period that most concerns us, for it was during this time that the Cumbrian stone circles were built. The transition between the early and later neolithic age is marked by a change in field monuments. In the south of England the last of the causewayed enclosures were constructed at this time; burial under long barrows and cairns gave way increasingly to burial under round mounds; and the early henge monuments and stone circles were being built. In Cumbria many of the round cairns and burial mounds that dot the fells belong to the later neolithic and early bronze age periods.

The onset of the later neolithic age in Cumbria is not marked by any apparent change in population. During this period settlement spread from the lower-lying regions into the higher land of the fells, land that up to this time had been tree-covered. The timing of the move to higher land is indicated by pollen analysis. Forest clearance around the head of Great Langdale, at a height of 400 m above sea-level, started during the first centuries of the 3rd millenium BC; and here there is evidence that fire was used for clearance, a method seemingly not used at the lowland sites.[8] Farther to the west, pollen analysis from Burnmoor Tarn (250 m above sea-level) shows that clearance began here during the early bronze age.[8] Still-visible results of land clearance within the fells are cairn-fields – areas of moorland containing many piles of stone, most of which probably had no sepulchral purpose. The cairn-field on Burnmoor is discussed later (p. 54), as it probably relates to the collection of stone circles there. A cairn-field on Barnscar, Stockdale Moor, was dated to the early bronze age from the find of small collared urns in one or two of the cairns.[30] More recently, radiocarbon dates averaging at 1705bc have been obtained from the cairn-field on Birrel Sike in the Calder Valley, west Cumbria.[31]

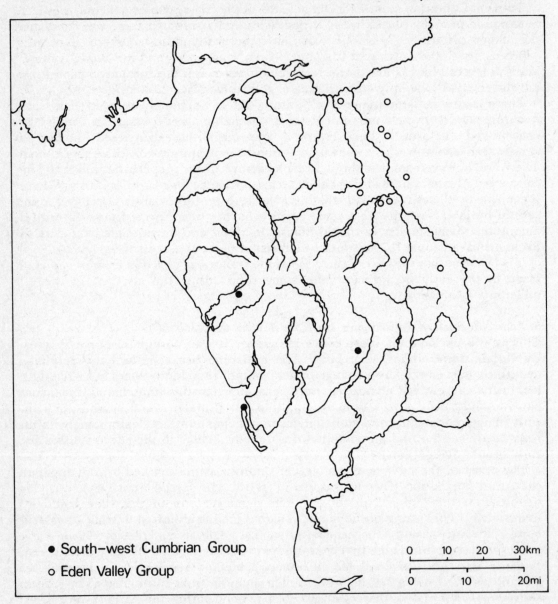

● South–west Cumbrian Group

○ Eden Valley Group

0   10   20   30km

0   10   20mi

Fig. 1.3 Distribution of Beakers in Cumbria, after T. H. McK. Clough.[33a]

The deforestation of the fells produced irreversible changes in soil-type and drainage, which eventually led to the spread of peat-bog. Like the coastal plain, the fells have remained treeless ever since.

The Cumbrian stone axe factories were still in production during the later neolithic period; but the making of stone axes probably ceased around 2300BC[32], at a time when bronze was first being used. The introduction of bronze from the Continent is associated with the so-called Beaker culture, which probably reached Cumbria around 1800-1900bc (2300-2400BC). The name of the culture derives from the finely made beaker-like pots, which were frequently placed in graves. The most common form of beaker burial is a crouched inhumation under a round mound. Many different types of beaker pottery are known, and it appears that their culture lasted throughout most of the early bronze age. In Cumbria, beakers have been found in the west and in the Eden valley[33a] (fig. 1.3). The western group is earlier; these beakers were decorated with parallel lines produced by twisted cord (fig. 1.4a). The beakers from the Eden valley area are typified by short necks (fig. 1.4b). Beaker people also favoured a new form of stone axe: the 'battle axe'. These implements have a round perforated hole through the body of the axe-head to take the shaft. The stone used in making the Cumbrian axes seems to be unsuitable for perforation, a fact that would have helped lead to the demise of the Cumbrian axe factories; however, at least one battle axe of Type VI rock is known.[13] Sites of possible beaker houses have been excavated at Woodhead near Bewcastle,[34] and in Levens Park in the far south of Cumbria.[35] These sites have produced evidence of habitation within a circular bank of stones. The Levens Park site also contained two burials, showing that it has more than a purely domestic significance.

The most common form of early bronze age pottery found in Cumbria is the collared urn. This type of vessel is usually associated with cremations, and they have been found in round cairns and stone circles throughout Cumbria. The diagnostic feature of collared urns is a wide overhanging rim, which often has an internal, decorated bevel. Urns can be decorated with a variety of impressed designs, but these are usually confined to the area above the widest part of the vessel (fig. 1.4c). The main purpose of collared urns appears to have been to contain cremated human bones and accompanying charcoal; and they are often found inverted over their contents. They seem to have been used throughout the early bronze age, perhaps to a later date than beakers. Collared urns are sometimes accompanied by much smaller vessels called pygmy (or incense) cups (fig. 1.4d). Their purpose is obscure – they almost certainly did not hold incense – but some have been found to contain calcined bone.

Food vessels form a third major class of early bronze age pottery found in Cumbria. Not as common as collared urns, they are concentrated along the Eden valley and near the north-west Cumbrian coast.[36] Several classes of food vessel are recognised; the most common form in northern England is the Yorkshire vase food vessel, named after the county in which they seem to have originated. Yorkshire vase food vessels are frequently decorated with impressed herringbone or similar design, and the vessels sometimes have lugs, which may be perforated, around the widest part of the body (fig. 1.4e). Whether they actually held food is unknown. Like

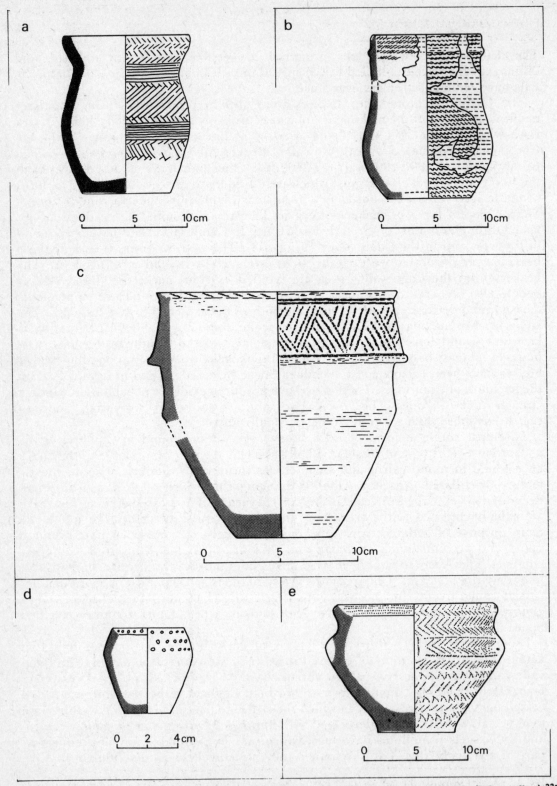

Fig. 1.4 Early bronze age pottery from Cumbria: a) Short-necked beaker from Ainstable (Eden valley);[33a] b) Cord-zoned beaker from Sizergh Fell (West Cumbria);[33a] c) Collared urn from Kirkoswald;[33b] d) Pygmy urn from near Barrow-in-Furness; e) Yorkshire vase food vessel from Shield Knowe, Bewcastle.[34]

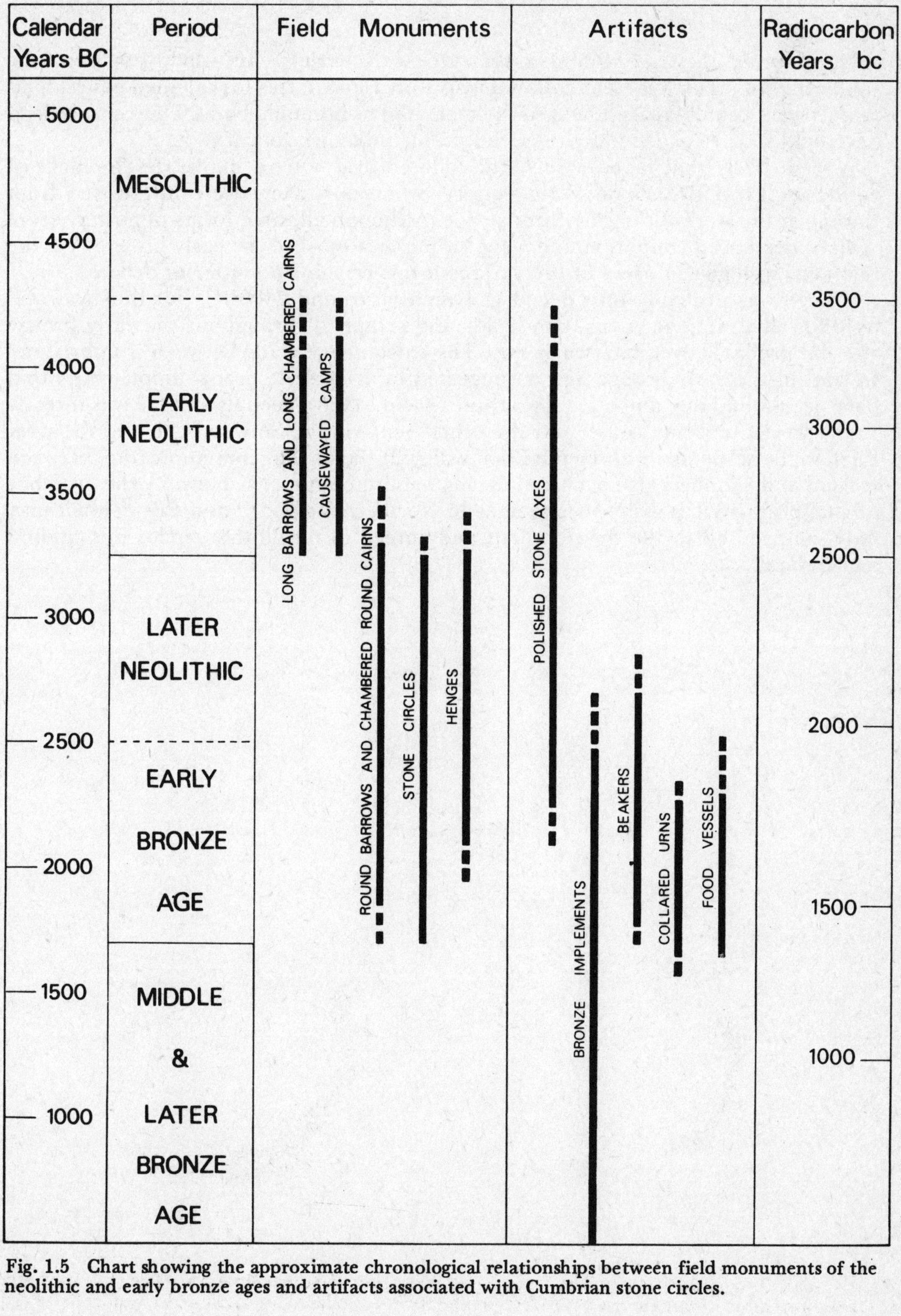

Calendar Years BC	Period	Field Monuments	Artifacts	Radiocarbon Years bc

Calendar Years BC: 5000, 4500, 4000, 3500, 3000, 2500, 2000, 1500, 1000

Period: MESOLITHIC, EARLY NEOLITHIC, LATER NEOLITHIC, EARLY BRONZE AGE, MIDDLE & LATER BRONZE AGE

Field Monuments: LONG BARROWS AND LONG CHAMBERED CAIRNS, CAUSEWAYED CAMPS, ROUND BARROWS AND CHAMBERED ROUND CAIRNS, STONE CIRCLES, HENGES

Artifacts: POLISHED STONE AXES, BRONZE IMPLEMENTS, BEAKERS, COLLARED URNS, FOOD VESSELS

Radiocarbon Years bc: 3500, 3000, 2500, 2000, 1500, 1000

Fig. 1.5   Chart showing the approximate chronological relationships between field monuments of the neolithic and early bronze ages and artifacts associated with Cumbrian stone circles.

collared urns, they are found associated with burials; but their function was somewhat different. Whereas collared urns were repositories for calcined bones, food vessels were usually placed next to the cremated or inhumed body. They may indeed have held food to accompany the dead on his unknown journey.

It seem likely that food vessels and collared urns were a native development of earlier styles of British neolithic pottery, whereas beakers were introduced from Europe at the start of the early bronze age. Although all three forms of pottery seem to have been used contemporaneously throughout most of the early bronze age, the relationship between users of the various forms remains a matter of debate.

Bronze was probably introduced to Cumbria around 2400BC, but flint was still used for small implements (arrowheads and scrapers) throughout the early bronze age and probably even later than this. The existence of trade between Cumbria and Ireland in the early bronze age is suggested by Irish-style bronze implements that have been found in Cumbria.[37] Two routes seem to have been used. One was directly to the west Cumbrian coast, and the other went via the Solway Firth and the river Eden to the settlements along the Eden valley. It seems that communication between Ireland and Cumbria also occurred during neolithic times, as shown by the presence of Cumbrian-style polished stone axes in Northern Ireland;[24] and this contact may have contributed to the development and spread of megalithic circles in Cumbria and Ireland.

Chapter Two

Cumbrian Stone Circles in Perspective

Introduction

In the British Isles, including Eire, a thousand or more sites described collectively as stone circles exist, or are known to have existed.[1] About sixty-five of them, or approximately a quarter of the stone circles in England, are to be found in Cumbria. Most of the Cumbrian circles are built on land adjacent to the central fells, i.e. the lower land in the west and south, and the hills adjoining the Eden valley in the east (fig. 3.1). Stone circles have a variety of shapes and forms; they were constructed over a period of two millenia or more; and they fulfilled differing functions. The Cumbrian circles include most of the types of stone circles to be found in the British Isles; and it seems likely that the Cumbrian circles vary in date from the earliest phase of the stone circle-building tradition (some time in the middle of the neolithic age, around 3200BC) to the end of the tradition (towards the end of the early bronze age, around 1600BC).

It is the purpose of this chapter to describe the various forms and shapes of stone circles, to discuss the possible reasons for which they were built, and to present evidence for the time-scale mentioned above.

Forms of Stone Circles and Related Monuments

The term 'stone circle' usually conjures up images of great monuments such as Castlerigg in Cumbria and Stanton Drew in Somerset: impressive rings of huge stones set about empty inner spaces. These are the truly 'megalithic' circles ('great stone' circles). However, for every circle of the grandeur of the Carles, Castlerigg, there are many lesser ones, little known and infrequently visited; yet these, too, are classed as stone circles. There are several types of these lesser circles, many of which are to be found in and around the Cumbrian Fells.

Several of the definitions below have been used by Frances Lynch to classify Welsh monuments;[2] and although they were only intended for the Welsh sites, they are equally applicable to some of the Cumbrian circles. It must be stressed that classification of circles according to the following categories is based purely on morphological character – how the circles appear today. It does not necessarily follow that there is a close cultural or chronological connection between circles in a

13

particular category. The present appearance of a circle can be misleading: a burial mound may have been placed within a circle long after the stones were raised, so changing the original purpose of the site; or the apparent absence of a burial mound might mean that a former mound has been either intentionally removed or has undergone denudation to the point of invisibility.

Of course, these definitions are ours; the circle-builders were ignorant of them.

Free-standing Stone Circles (fig. 2.1a)

These consist of a circle of stones set in the ground without any containing or surrounding bank. This category can be divided into two classes. Open stone circles have a featureless inner area with no evidence of burial. Most of the megalithic circles in England are of this type. Cumbrian examples are the Carles, Castlerigg and Swinside.

Some Cumbrian free-standing stone circles surround a burial mound (or mounds) having a diameter of less than half that of the stone circle. In this second class are Grey Croft and the Burnmoor circles in west Cumbria.

Concentric Stone Circles (fig. 2.1b)

These are a relatively uncommon form, consisting of two stone circles with a common, or nearly common, centre. Only about thirty are known in Great Britain.[3] A small number of them are to be found in Cumbria; perhaps the best known of these is the Druids' Circle on Birkrigg.

Embanked Stone Circles (fig. 2.1c)

In this type of monument a ring of large standing stones is surrounded by, or forms the inner face of, a penannular bank of earth or small stones. The only complete example in Cumbria is Gamelands; but the great open circle of Long Meg and her Daughters has the remains of a bank on its western perimeter. The appearance of embanked stone circles suggests a relationship with circle-henges (see below).

Cairn Circles (fig. 2.1d)

Frances Lynch defines these as comprising a low cairn, in which prominent standing stones are set near the perimeter.[2] Several circles of this type are in the Eden valley region of east Cumbria.

Embanked Circles (fig. 2.1e)

There are a number of ring monuments in Cumbria marked on the Ordnance Survey maps simply as 'circles'; they are described elsewhere as 'stone circles', but they do not fall within any of the above categories. They consist of a penannular bank of earth and stones surrounding a flat or slightly domed interior, and they have larger stones standing above the level of the bank. The Beacon circle near Lowick and the Banniside circle near Coniston are examples of this class.

These circles might be included within Lynch's definition of a 'ring cairn': a bank of stone surrounding a hollow central area;[2] however, the term 'ring cairn' has been used by other authors to describe somewhat different structures. Burl, when applying

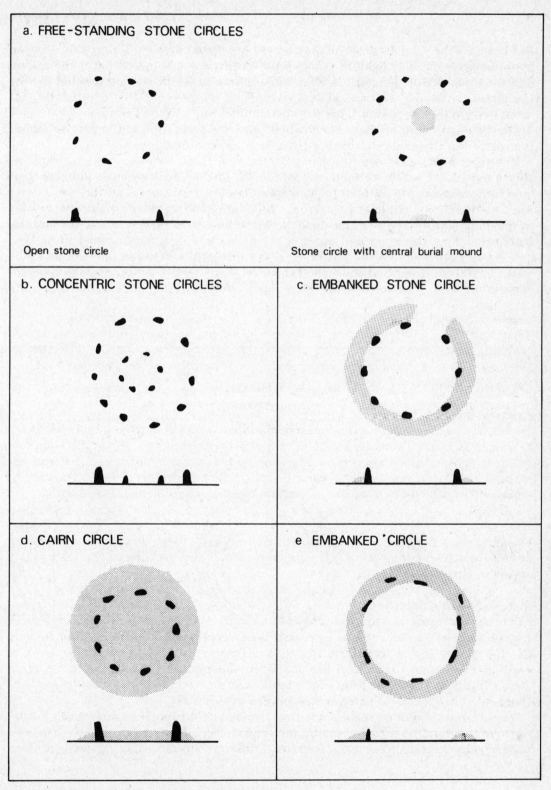

Fig. 2.1 Stone circles and related monuments.

the term to the Clava cairns of north-east Scotland, defines a ring cairn as 'an approximately circular bank of stones with a central space that is never more than half the diameter of the cairn itself'.[4] This definition is clearly not suitable for the Cumbrian sites. Excavation of the Banniside circle (p. 80) revealed several interments in the inner area. This site and similar circles in the Pennines, where they are particularly common, have been called 'enclosed cremation cemeteries'[5] – a term that describes their function rather than their appearance.

In order to overcome the problem of definition, Cumbrian sites with a profile as shown in fig. 2.1e will be termed *embanked circles*. The term is chosen to indicate their structural relationship with embanked stone circles. Links between the two classes are provided by the circle at Casterton, which has small, regularly-placed stones set in the bank, and by the Cockpit near the Moor Divock circles, where a low circular bank is faced on the inner and outer edges with standing stones up to 1 m high.

It is fairly obvious that there is no clear-cut distinction between the various forms of stone circle as described above, and the term 'ring-work' has been used to cover all classes:[6] at one extreme are the great open stone circles, and at the other the embanked circles.

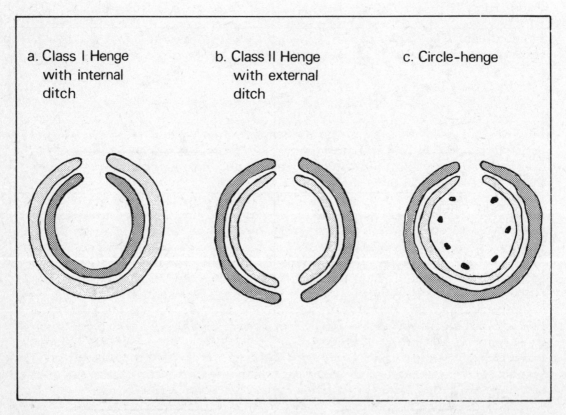

a. Class I Henge
   with internal
   ditch

b. Class II Henge
   with external
   ditch

c. Circle-henge

Fig. 2.2   Henge monuments.

Henges (fig. 2.2)

Henges are considered to be closely related to the great stone circles. They consist of a roughly circular area enclosed by a bank usually with an associated ditch. They occur throughout the British Isles, but are found more commonly in the east and south – i.e. away from the main highland regions. Henge monuments are divided into two classes, defined by the number of entrances in the bank. Class I henges (fig. 2.2a) have one entrance; class II henges (fig. 2.2b) have two or more. Their sizes vary from that of the diminutive example of Fargo Plantation in Wiltshire (diameter 10.6 m), to that of the great, village-enclosing henge of Avebury, also in Wiltshire, whose irregular bank has an average diameter exceeding 350 m. Avebury actually belongs to a class of monument that combines a henge and a stone circle: a circle-henge (fig. 2.2c). The immense sarsen stones forming the stone circles within the bank and ditch of Avebury have been sadly much reduced over the centuries by wilful destruction; but enough stones of the outer circle remain to impress upon us the great task undertaken by the builders.

There are only two certain henges remaining in Cumbria: King Arthur's Round Table and Mayburgh, within half a kilometre (½ mile) of each other just to the south of Penrith. The Round Table is a class II henge, but its second entrance was destroyed by road-widening at the end of the 19th century. Mayburgh is unusual in having no ditch; it is a class I henge with an immense bank composed of cobbles. It should probably be classed as a circle-henge, because there are historical records of a circle of standing stones inside the bank. Of these, only a single, tall stone remains.

The Shapes and Construction of Stone Circles

It is often not apparent, even to the careful observer, that many stone circles are not laid out on the ground as true circles; their geometrical forms only become obvious when accurately surveyed plans are studied. The seeming lack of logic in using the term 'stone circle' to describe these non-circular structures has led several writers to use the term 'stone ring'; but the term 'stone circle' is so familiar and widely used, that it will be retained here.

The most important and influential contribution to the study of the geometry and shapes of stone circles has been made by Alexander Thom. Over several decades his careful surveys and studies of stone circles of all forms throughout Great Britain, including some 15 in Cumbria, have led him to propose far-reaching suggestions for their construction and use. He has defined four main categories of shape:[7] circle, flattened circle, ellipse and egg (fig. 2.3). There are two main sorts of flattened circle (Type A and Type B), differing in their geometrical construction. A third type of flattened circle (Type D) is a slight variation on Type A. The egg-shaped rings are also divided into two classes – Type I and Type II; and later, Thom added a third type of egg.[8] A fifth category, the compound ring, refers to a few sites that have more complicated geometries, such as the Avebury henge; there is no known stone circle in Cumbria in this category. Of the stone circles in the British Isles, Burl has calculated that there are 600 circles, 150 flattened circles, 100 ellipses and 50 eggs.[9]

The easiest shape to construct would have been the circle, which would have required only a central peg and a length of cord to scribe out the perimeter on the

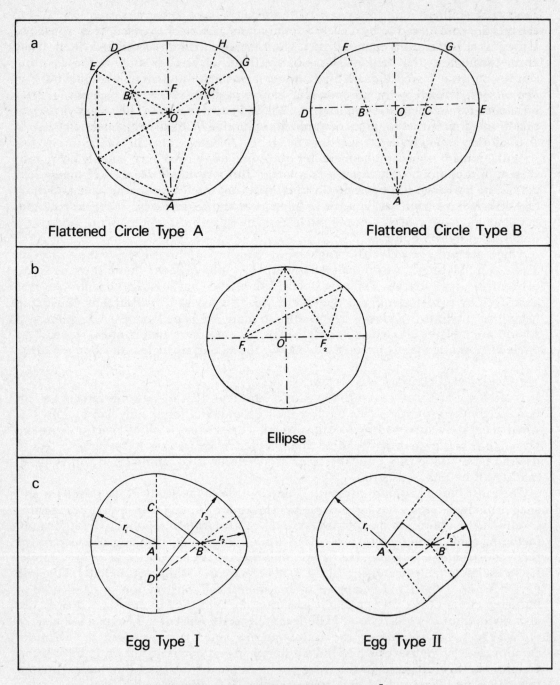

Fig. 2.3 Methods of construction of non-circular rings, after Thom.[7]
a) Flattened Circle Types A and B. Arcs are struck from the following centres: Type A: O(arc EAG),
A (arc DH), B (arc ED), C (arc HG); Type B: O (arc DAE), A (arc FG), B (arc DF), C (arc GE).
b) Ellipse: anchor points are at foci F_1 and F_2.
c) Egg-shaped Circles Types I and II. Arcs are struck from the following centres: Type I: A, B, C and
D; Type II: A and B.

ground. An ellipse could be drawn fairly simply using two fixed stakes at the foci of the ellipse, with a loop of cord passed round them. A scriber would then mark out the ellipse as it was moved round against the taut loop. The constructions of flattened circles and eggs would have been much more difficult, and Thom's schemes (fig. 2.3) imply that the circle builders possessed a surprisingly advanced knowledge of geometry, probably empirically based. In scribing out these shapes using Thom's methods, the various arcs of the circumference are centred on key points, the positions of which have to be determined beforehand. In the eggs, a knowledge of Pythagorean triangles is required.

If the circle-builders took so much care in designing their rings, one wonders why they were apparently so careless in placing the individual stones. Frequently the stones are scattered haphazardly around the reconstructed perimeter, as can be seen from Thom's plan of the Type A flattened circle of Brat's Hill (Burnmoor E) (fig. 2.4).

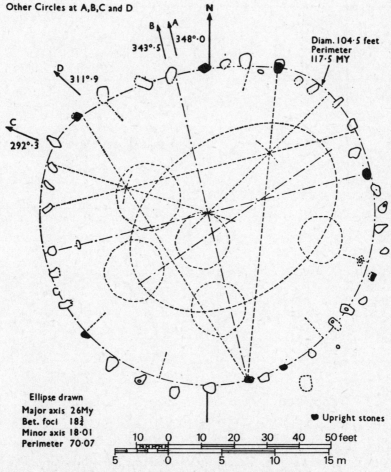

Fig. 2.4 Brat's Hill (Burnmoor E), after Thom (ref. 7, p. 60).

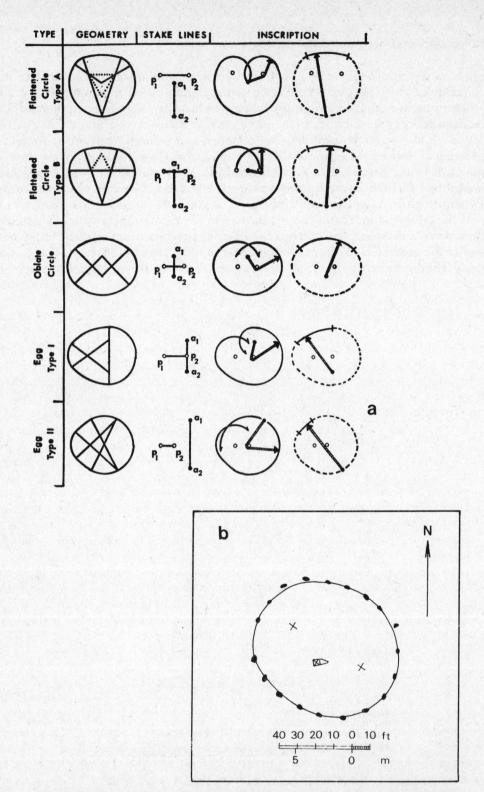

Fig. 2.5 Other methods of construction of non-circular rings: a) Construction of shapes of stone rings according to Cowan[14] (copyright 1970 by the AAAS); b) Angell's construction of Boscawen-un stone circle using three anchor points.[15]

Thom's typology is not meant to imply any chronological sequence. The question of the relative dating of the shapes is dealt with more fully later, but it is worth mentioning here that circles and flattened circles are likely to be earlier in date than ellipses and eggs.

From a statistical analysis of the dimensions of stone circles and other megalithic sites in the British Isles, Thom has argued persuasively that these structures were designed using a standard unit of length. He calls this unit the Megalithic Yard (MY) (1 MY = 2.72ft or 0.83m), and he claims that it was in use from one end of Britain to the other with an accuracy of 1 per cent or greater.[7] Stone circles were constructed preferably so that their diameters were whole numbers of MYs, and their circumferences multiples of 2½ MYs. The claims for the megalithic yard have not received general acceptance; Burl describes the country-wide megalithic yard as a 'chimera, a gross statistical misconception'.[10] It may be that the rings were set out using a body-based unit such as the pace or the distance between people holding hands. The proposed accuracy of the megalithic yard may simply be an accurate average of a naturally varying unit. It is beyond the scope of this book to consider the several counter-arguments to Thom's claims. There are a number of excellent reviews available that discuss the statistical evidence in detail; particularly useful are book by Lancaster-Brown,[11] Heggie[12] and MacKie.[13]

Thom is not alone in suggesting shapes and designs for stone circles, but recent ideas owe a good deal to Thom's pioneering work. Cowan[14] has defined five non-circular shapes: flattened circles Types A and B, oblate circle (in place of Thom's ellipse), and eggs Types I and II (fig. 2.5a). The shapes are very similar to, but not identical with, Thom's; however, the proposed methods of construction are much simpler, and they all rely on a similar technique. The only requirements are two fixed posts p_1 and p_2, and a length of cord, one end of which is fixed at either point *a* or at point *b*. Constructions are shown graphically in fig. 2.5. Yet another means of constructing Thom's shapes has been suggested by Angell. Like Cowan's method, it is simpler than Thom's; and all the shapes can be drawn out by passing a loop around three[15] or four[16] stakes. Angell's interpretation of the shape of Boscawen-Un stone circle in Cornwall is shown in fig. 2.5b. It is interesting to note that the position of one of the stakes is that of a tall standing stone, now leaning, within the circle. The fact that these three incompatible methods give good fits to the same sites should ring a warning bell against making assumptions about the actual methods used. Angell has warned of the 'ever-present danger of projecting the experience of modern mathematics and technology onto the artefacts of what must be considered an alien culture'.[15]

Uses of Stone Circles

a) 'Ceremony and Burial'

It is possible to divide all stone circles into two groups: those for which there is no firm evidence for burials within the circle, and those that contain burials or at least deposits of human bone. Both groups occur throughout the British Isles. In England the average diameter of the open stone circle containing no burial (25.7 m.) is greater than that of the burial circles (14.5 m.).[19] It is the great megalithic circles of Cumbria, Wiltshire and the south-west of England for which there is no evidence of their use as funerary monuments. Even when excavations have been carried out at these great open circles, few, if any, artifacts have been found to help explain their significance. It is obvious that such monuments, requiring great organization and labour to build, must have possessed a purpose of great value for the communities that raised them; and for no other reason than a lack of a reasonable alternative, they are generally regarded as having had some combination of ceremonial and ritual function. Their possible use as 'astronomical observatories' has provoked much discussion recently, and this aspect is discussed in the next section.

It is not known whether great circles like Castlerigg were built for the exclusive use of the local community, or whether they had a wider cultural significance. They may have been places at which people from a wide area assembled at certain times of the year. Perhaps people came together to trade goods, to arrange marriages and to indulge in ritual celebration. The association in folklore of stone circles with dancing may be a dim memory of such festivities. From the Merry Maidens stone circle in Cornwall comes the legend of 19 maidens turned to stone for dancing on Sunday. The circle's alternative name, Dawn's Men, is not an attempt at megalithic sexual equality, but a corruption of the Cornish *Dans Maen* – stone dance.

Goods that may have been traded at the stone circles are polished stone axes. A country-wide distribution of stone axes certainly did take place (p. 7). It seems that they were regarded not simply as tools, but were used as cult objects as well; that is, they had some ritual significance,[20] and practices connected with such a cult may well have taken place within the open stone circles. Henges may have served the same function. Evidence for an 'axe-cult' is provided by what appears to be the ritual placing of axes inside a number of stone circles and henges. A polished stone axe was found buried blade-downwards in the Llandegai henge in Gwynedd; a broken stone axe was discovered buried by one of the stones of the Grey Croft circle in Cumbria; and 'model' axes made of chalk have been found at Stonehenge and Woodhenge. To quote Burl: 'A place where axes were bartered would not only be a meeting place but a temple in which trade and ritual went hand in hand'.[9]

The smaller, burial circles in Cumbria are of several types. There are cairn-circles (fig. 2.1d), free-standing stone circles surrounding a burial cairn (fig. 2.1a), and embanked circles (fig. 2.1e); in some of the small circles, burials may lie beneath a now-level interior. The burials in these Cumbrian circles consist frequently of deposits of calcined bone and charcoal placed in pits, sometimes accompanied by or contained in a pottery vessel – either a collared urn or a food vessel.

Although there is an obvious difference between a megalithic ring like Castlerigg and small burial circles like the cairn-circles on Moor Divock in east Cumbria, one should be careful not to place too much significance on the distinction between 'ceremonial' and 'burial' circles. R. G. Collingwood was the first to classify the Cumbrian open stone circles as a group distinct from the smaller circles containing burials. He termed them 'great circles', and he considered them to have been used for seasonal festivals and in the distribution of stone axes.[21] He defined them as consisting of large stones not surrounding a tumulus, and he listed 16 or so of them:

Elva Plain, Blakeley Raise (Kinniside), Grey Croft, Mayburgh, Long Meg and her Daughters, Kemp Howe (Shap), Gamelands, Swinside, Castlerigg, Egremont, Grey Yauds, Motherby, Rawthey Bridge, Hall Foss, Annaside and Ash House Wood. It is doubtful, however, if many of these fall strictly within his definition. The latter seven no longer exist; so their original nature is uncertain; and others are now known to have contained burials. On excavation, Grey Croft was found to contain a burial cairn; and a burial mound is visible within Blakeley Raise. Even such sites as Castlerigg may contain insignificant burials. It is also possible that the burial cairns in Grey Croft, Brat's Hill and Gunnerkeld may not have been there originally; they may indicate some change in function of these circles. With so little information to go on, it is impossible to draw an accurate picture of their original purpose.

Even the smaller burial circles may have had some ritual function. It is apparent that these circles were not used as cemeteries for general burials by the local population: there are too few interments in each circle for this; and often the individual cremated deposits do not contain the remains of complete skeletons. Whatever the burial practices were, it therefore seems possible that at least some were involved in the ritual, and the deposits of bone had a significance other than that of simple burial. Crushed human bone found under the stones of the Broomrigg C circle in Cumbria has been interpreted as a 'foundation sacrifice'.[22] Outside Cumbria more direct evidence for ritual burial has been discovered. At the Druids' Circle near Penmaenmawr in Gwynedd the cremated bones of children were found. The sad remains have been described as 'dedications, offerings of death for the sake of the living'.[23] Also in Wales, the decapitated body of a child was buried in a circle at Aber Cwmddyr in Dyfed.[2]

b) Astronomy

The notion that megalithic circles were used in making astronomical observations has been current for a century or more; but it is mainly due to the meticulous and rigorous work of Alexander Thom, with the aid of his son and grandson, that the subject of astro-archaeology (or archaeo-astronomy, as it is sometimes called) has become a subject of serious discussion among professional archaeologists.

What sort of astronomical observations might the megalith-builder have made? Most probably they would have been the rising and setting of the sun, the moon, or bright stars. It is claimed that the positions on the horizon of these risings and settings were indicated by alignments between two standing stones or between a stone and a distant natural foresight. Stone circles are not the only type of monument that may have been used for this purpose; claims have also been made for other megalithic sites, such as menhirs (single standing stones) and chambered cairns.

Stonehenge, not unnaturally, has attracted more attention as a possible 'megalithic observatory' than have other stone circles; and much theorizing has been conducted on its possible use in monitoring the motions of the sun and moon, and in predicting eclipses. But these ideas have not been generally accepted. Thom's great contribution, apart from his methodical approach, has been in extending the study to a large number of lesser megalithic monuments throughout Great Britain, including some sites in Brittany. Although these sites may be architecturally less impressive than Stonehenge, if Thom's claims for them are true, many of them may have a greater astronomical significance.

It is not the purpose of this short section to discuss Thom's work in detail, nor to discuss the careful criticisms of his analyses that have been published.[11, 12, 13] But a brief survey of Thom's results will be given, as some of the circles he has studied are in Cumbria.

Thom has published his results in three books and several papers. The astronomical alignments considered in his first book[7] are mostly those concerned with the sun and certain bright stars, and only a few relate to the moon. He suggests that the solar observations allowed 'megalithic man' to construct a calendar. The solstices and equinoxes divide the year into four approximately equal parts. The times of the solstices could have been determined by noting the days on which the sun had its maximum northerly (for the summer solstice) or its maximum southerly (for the winter solstice) rising and setting positions. The equinoxes occur midway between the solstices. These are the days on which the sun rises and sets in the same positions in spring and autumn. These points on the local horizon were probably found by trial and error; but once they had been found, they would be indicated by alignments, as also were the solsticial rising and setting positions. Thom claims also to have found evidence for a 16-fold division of the year, but the statistical evidence for this appears to be weak.[12]

His second[24] and third[8] books are concerned largely with observations of the moon. The rising and setting points of the sun on the horizon change through one year from its maximum northern to its maximum southern position and back again. In contrast, the motion of the moon is much more complex. The moon's orbit is inclined to that of the earth, and the sun imposes a slight perturbation to its motion. In consequence, the moon goes through its cycle of extreme maximum rising and setting positions over a period of 18.6 years. In his second book, Thom presents evidence that these extreme positions could be detected at a number of 'megalithic lunar observatories'.

Thom lists only a few stone circles among his lunar observatories; most of the observatory sites are menhirs used in conjunction with a distant foresight – usually a 'notch' on a hillside on the local horizon. Such a long line-of-sight would be required to provide the great accuracy needed to detect the extreme lunar positions. Among the stone circles included are Stonehenge and the Scottish circles of Brodgar, Callanish and Temple Wood. In fact, Thom's work indicates that stone circles were not themselves built as observatories. In cases where Thom has found significant astronomical alignments involving stone circles, the alignments are seldom between pairs of circle stones; rather, they are between pairs of adjacent circles as at Burnmoor in Cumbria, or between a circle and an outlying stone. Referring to stone circles, Thom states that 'in only one or two examples were the spacings and orientation (of the stones) controlled by the desire to indicate the rising or setting positions of the sun or moon at important times';[8a] and even more damningly: 'most of them (stone circles) have no astronomical significance'.[8b] There are one or two exceptions, however; one of them is the Carles, Castlerigg, the construction of which has built into it solar and possibly lunar alignments (p. 97).

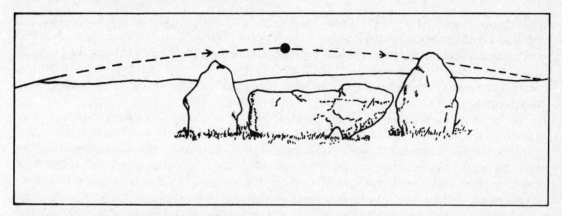

Fig. 2.6   Reconstruction of the apparent motion of the moon at its extreme southerly position as seen from within Aikey Brae, after Burl.[25]

Many stone circles certainly contain indicators for some fundamental orientations: some have tall stones or entrances in northerly or southerly positions; some definitely seem to have solsticial or equinoctal alignments built into them. But these things do not make them observatories. More likely, such alignments would be purely symbolic or perhaps concerned with ritual, just as many churches are orientated towards the rising point of the sun on a particular saint's day.

A good illustration of the possible connection between a circle's orientation and associated ritual is provided by Burl's analysis of the recumbent stone circles* in north-east Scotland.[25] The recumbent stones of many of them are set towards the south. To anyone standing within such a circle, the moon, when at its extreme southerly position, would have seemed to drift along the very top of the recumbent (fig. 2.6). Would this have been the occasion for some ritual practice, among the long, pale, moon-cast shadows of the stones? Perhaps; but alas, this is pure speculation.

c) Mystical Associations

A picture of a landscape permeated by a mysterious force (an 'earth-force') is drawn in several books and articles. The lines of force have been associated with 'ley-lines' and astronomical alignments. It is claimed that the megalith builders were conscious of these spectral manifestations, and they built their stone circles at places where lines of force intersected; this force can be detected today by dowsers and natural sensitives. The holders of this image of the past have a two-fold problem in proving their case: not only has this supposed force to be identified, but evidence has to be shown for the purposeful association of megalithic monuments with the force.

Two recently published sets of results may have some relevance here. Measurements using a Geiger counter, carried out by members of the 'Dragon Project', revealed anomalous levels of radiation inside the stone circles of the Merry Maidens

*Recumbent stone circles are unknown in Cumbria, but frequently occur in north-east Scotland. They comprise a circle of free-standing stones, with the two tallest stones flanking a large, level-topped recumbent stone.

in Cornwall and Moel Ty Uchaf in Gwynedd.[26] A magnetometer survey of the
Rollright Stones in Oxfordshire showed regions of reduced magnetic field within the
circle; these regions formed a spiral pattern, the centre of which was the mid-point of
the circle.[27] But what do these results mean? The measured anomalies may be the
passive results of the stones themselves; megalithic man may have been no more
aware of them than a visitor to the circles today.

Having considered the possible uses for stone circles, can any conclusions be
drawn? All that can be said is that they probably fulfilled several functions: for
holding public ceremonies; for conducting rituals, possibly involving the sun or the
moon; and for burial. The funebrial aspect would be more important in some circles
than in others. A good analogy is a medieval cathedral. Not only were religious
services conducted there; people were buried beneath its floor; the nave was an area
in which people could meet and talk; marriages and other ceremonies were carried
out within it; and the axis of the building would be aligned towards the rising sun.

The Dating of Cumbrian Stone Circles

a) The Methods

Dating is a problem that is common to all the stone circles of the British Isles. The
most direct method of dating is by carbon-14 analysis, which is determined from
organic remains found during excavation. Unfortunately, few circles have been dated
by this method. Among those that have, the earliest date so far obtained is from
Newgrange in County Meath, Eire. The site consists of a great ring of stones of
diameter just over 100 m, which encircles a spectacular chambered cairn. A
radiocarbon date of 2550±45bc (about 3300BC) was obtained from within the cairn,
and it has been convincingly argued that the circle is as old as, if not older than, the
cairn.[28] Other circles that have radiocarbon dates are: Stenness (Orkney),
2238±70bc and 2356±65bc; Barbrook II (Derbyshire), 1500±150bc; Berrybrae
(Grampian) 1500±80bc and 1360±90bc; and the latest date so far recorded,
1200±150bc, for the circle at Sandy Road, Scone (Tayside). Although the sites dated
by this method are a very small fraction of the total number of stone circles, the
results obtained probably give a range of dates in which the other circles can be
placed. It is therefore reasonable to assume that stone circles were being built in the
British Isles from the start of the later neolithic to the end of the early bronze age, a
period of some two millenia (fig. 1.5).

Attempts have been made to date certain circles by an astronomical method. Two
phenomena have been used for this purpose: the precession of the equinoxes and the
changing obliquity of the ecliptic. The first of these effects causes the rising point of a
star on the horizon to change slowly with time. If an alignment of stones is known
with certainty to point to the rising of a particular star, the date at which the star rose
at the position indicated can be calculated. Using this method, Thom has suggested
a date of 1900-1800BC for the Burnmoor circles, based on an alignment to Arcturus.[7]
On the whole, such dating should be accepted only reservedly. Thom[8c] states that the

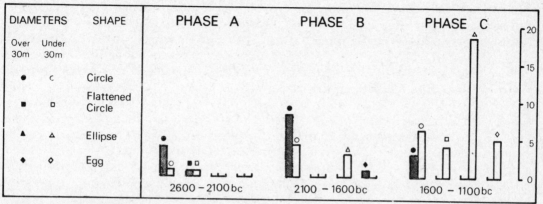

Fig. 2.7 Histogram of shapes and phases of megalithic rings. The radio-carbon dates are derived from artefacts found within the rings, after Burl.[30]

method is disappointing, as it is impossible to be absolutely certain of the association of a given alignment with a definite star.

The changing obliquity of the ecliptic causes the sun's rising point at the summer solstice to be shifted slightly farther to the south each year. The effect is only very small, about one degree (or twice the apparent diameter of the sun) every 4300 years. But if an alignment is known to denote the rising point of the sun at the summer solstice, the date of its use can be determined. By this means, Lockyer predicted a date of approximately 1700BC for the main construction of Stonehenge.[29] Again, much caution is needed in accepting a date obtained by this method. Choosing the part of the sun used in the observations (upperlimb, lower limb, or centre) can alter the calculated date by up to 2000 years.[11]

For the majority of stone circles direct dating must be obtained from artifacts, the most useful being pottery associated with burials. Dating by this technique is by no means precise, as many pottery types were in use for several centuries (see fig. 1.5). By using this method, Burl has shown that it is possible to place the shapes of stone rings very approximately in a chronological order:[9, 30] circle; flattened circle; ellipse; egg.

A more detailed analysis of the results is shown in fig. 2.7. In the earliest phase (phase A) are circles and flattened circles; in phase B eggs and ellipses first appear, and these predominate in phase C. It can also be seen that as the age of the ring increases, so does its average diameter. The earliest rings are therefore likely to be the largest. Other useful generalizations are that large stones precede small ones and, at least for English sites, circles that contain burials are expected to be later than those that do not; but it must be borne in mind that a circle may predate a burial that it surrounds by a considerable period. Burl also lists clearly marked entrances, outliers, and close spacing of stones[31] as properties of the earliest stone circles.

b) The Early Circles
The great, open Cumbrian stone circles have some, if not all, of these early traits, and Burl suggests that among them may be the first stone circles raised in Great Britain.[1]

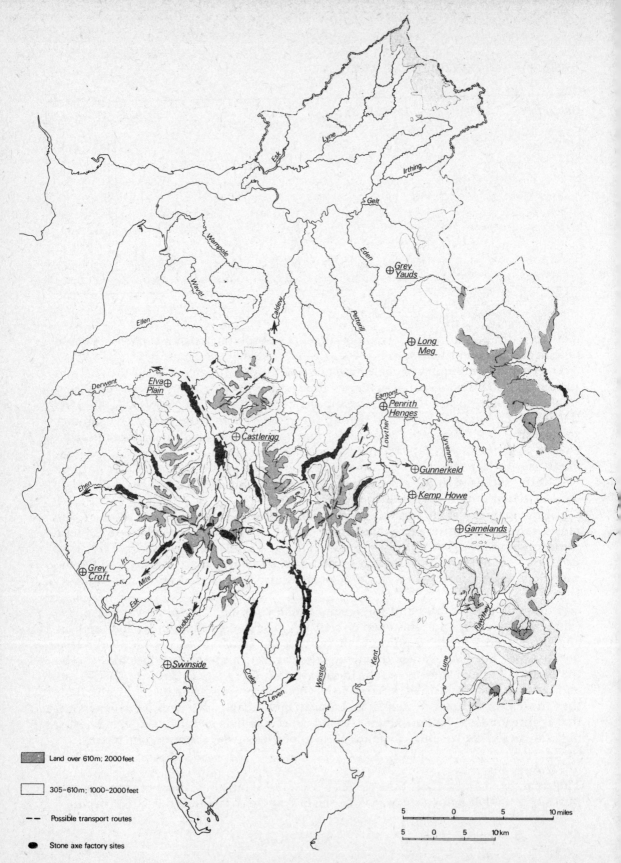

Land over 610m; 2000 feet

305–610m; 1000–2000 feet

Possible transport routes

Stone axe factory sites

Fig. 2.8 Routes through the fells used for the distribution of roughed-out stone axes from the factory sites, after Plint (Ch. 1, ref. 21).

Long Meg and her Daughters, Swinside and Castlerigg are obvious members of the group; and others may be Grey Croft, Kemp Howe, Elva Plain, the destroyed Grey Yauds, and the circle-henge of Mayburgh.

There is virtually no artifactual evidence from excavation to verify an early date for these circles. What is consistent with their construction in mid to late neolithic times is the evidence that they were connected with the distribution of stone axes from the Great Langdale and other factory sites in the fells. Even before the discovery of the factory sites, R. G. Collingwood suggested that the builders of the great circles were also the users of the stone axes (p. 22). He was led to this belief by the similarity in location of these stone circles and stray finds of stone axes. Carbon-14 dating of a chipping site near the Great Langdale factory (p. 5) shows that axe-making was taking place here around the middle of the 3rd millenium bc, a date in keeping with the postulated time-scale for the early circles.

After the axes had been chipped to the desired shapes at the factory sites, they were taken away for grinding and polishing. The finishing sites seem to have been away from the fells, and may have been where the factory workers had their settlements. Ehenside Tarn is the best-documented example (p. 4). The routes used to transport the rough-outs have been deduced from stray finds of flakes and unfinished axes. These routes are shown in fig. 2.8, together with those circles considered early on architectural grounds; the henges of Arthur's Round Table and Mayburgh are also included. Many of the circles are in locations where the routes leave the higher fells for the lower land; and Burl has pointed out that the juxtaposition of circle and axe-route lends support to Collingwood's original suggestion.[32]

There is no evidence that the polishing or grinding of axes was carried out within the circles themselves; but several of the circles in fig. 2.8 are close to places where collections of rough-outs and sometimes grinding equipment have been found. At Portinscale, at the north end of Derwent Water and near to Castlerigg, several rough-outs and incompletely polished axes were found, suggesting that this was a finishing site.[33] The possible finishing site at Clifton is near Mayburgh,[33] and that at Kell Bank near Gosforth is close to Grey Croft (p. 64). At Hunsonby, to the south of the great circle of Long Meg, two rough-outs were discovered in 1884.[34] Stone axes have actually been found in three of the circles. A broken polished axe comes from Grey Croft (p. 64), and there are reported discoveries of unpolished axes from inside Castlerigg (p. 97) and Mayburgh (p. 149).

As suggested earlier, it may be possible that these circles served as markets from which traders would take the finished axes to many parts of the British Isles. The western circles such as Swinside and Grey Croft are well positioned to have been involved in the export of axes to the Isle of Man and Ireland. The more distant circles of Long Meg and Grey Yauds are on a route that could have supplied axes to southern Scotland and to north-east England via the Tyne Gap (p. 7).

It may seem something of a mystery that while Cumbria has many megalithic circles, it seems to have been virtually ignored by the builders of megalithic tombs. There is in fact only one possible megalithic tomb in the county, in the village of Great Urswick near Ulverston. But the economic importance of the region at the time

Early Stone Circles of Later Neolithic Date

Later Stone Circles of Early Bronze-Age Date

Open Stone Circles	Embanked Stone Circles	Free-standing Stone Circles around a Burial or Mound	Concentric Stone Circles	Cairn Circles	Embanked Circles	Very Small Open Stone Circles
Castlerigg	Gamelands	Brat's Hill[b]	Birkrigg[a]	Little Meg	Beacon	Bleaberry Haws
Swinside		Low Longrigg[b] NE and SW	Hird Wood?	Moor Divock 4[a]	Banniside[a]	White Hag
Elva Plain		White Moss[b] NE and SW	Oddendale	Moor Divock 5[a]	Casterton	Castlehowe Scar
Kemp Howe		Blakeley Raise		Leacet Hill[a]	Kirk	
Long Meg and her Daughters		Lacra B		Broomrigg B		
		Lacra D[a]		Broomrigg C[a]		
				Iron Hill S		

a. early bronze-age pottery found
b. other evidence for an early bronze-age date

Fig. 2.9   Classification of some Cumbrian stone circles and their relative chronologies.

when the great circles were built, as attested by the nationwide distribution of Cumbrian axes, would have provided the necessary initiative and resources to raise the circles.

c) The Later Circles

The majority of stone circles in Cumbria have architectural features that indicate a later date for these circles than for the early circles discussed above. Their diameters and the heights of their stones are generally less than those of the early circles; several of them are ellipses; and at least one, Leacet Hill, is an egg. Moreover, there is artifactual evidence for an early bronze age date for these circles. Many, if not all, of the later circles were used for burial, either under a cairn or a now-level interior; and where pottery has been found associated with the burials, it is always of early bronze age type. It is therefore likely that all these later circles belong to the early bronze age.

Figure 2.9 shows a relative chronology for some Cumbrian stone circles according to their forms and based on the dating methods outlined above. It must be stressed that the placing of circles on the chart in fig. 2.9 is only tentative. Modifications will almost certainly need to be made as further evidence becomes available.

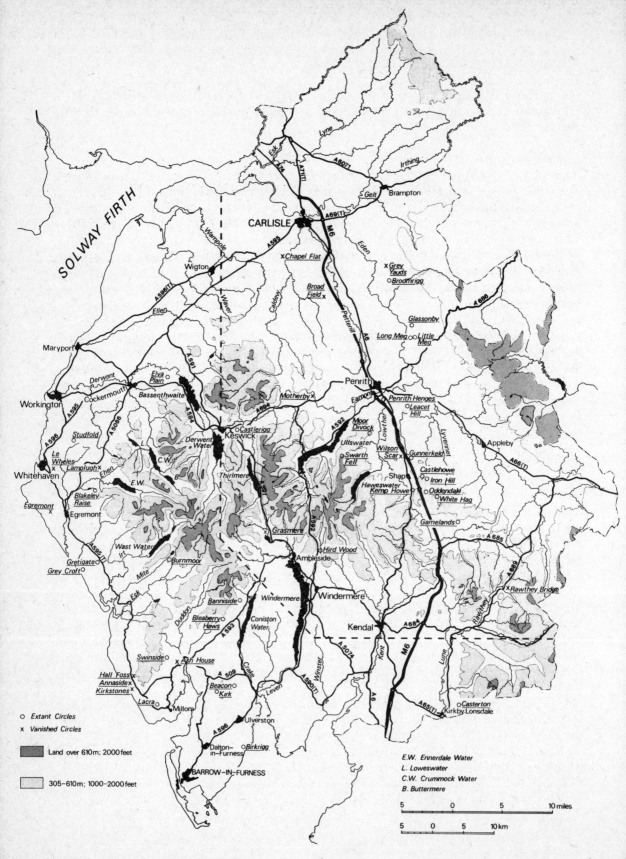

Fig. 3.1 Locations of stone circles in Cumbria.

Map labels (clockwise / by region):

SOLWAY FIRTH

Lyne
Esk
A74
A7(T)
A6071
Irthing
Gelt
Brampton
A69(T)
CARLISLE
M6
A595
Chapel Flat
Eden
Grey Yauds
Broomrigg
Wampole
Wigton
Caldew
Broad Field
Glassonby
Petteril
A596(T)
Ellen
Waver
Long Meg
Little Meg
A686
Maryport
A591
A6
Penrith
Derwent
Elva Plain
Bassenthwaite
Penrith Henges
Cockermouth
Eamont
A5086
A66(T)
Workington
A595
Motherby
Leacet Hill
Moor Divock
Lowther
Studfold
A594
Castlerigg
Keswick
Ullswater
Appleby
Lyvennet
Le Wheles
Lamplugh
L.
C.W.
Derwent Water
Swarth Fell
Wilson Scar
Gunnerkeld
A66(T)
Whitehaven
A596
Ehen
B.
Thirlmere
Shap
Castlehowe
Iron Hill
Blakeley Raise
E.W.
Haweswater
Kemp Howe
Oddendale
White Hag
Egremont
Egremont
Gamelands
A685
Wast Water
Irt
A593
Grasmere
A592
Hird Wood
A595(T)
Gretigate
Burnmoor
Ambleside
Rawthey Bridge
Grey Croft
Mite
Esk
Duddon
Banniside
Windermere
Windermere
A685
A683
Bleaberry Haws
Coniston Water
Kendal
A684
M6
Swinside
Ash House
A593
Crake
Winster
Kent
A507A
Rawthey
Hall Foss
Annaside
Kirkstones
A595(T)
A509
Beacon Kirk
Leven
A590(T)
A6
Lune
Lacra
Millom
A65(T)
Casterton
Kirkby Lonsdale
A595
Ulverston
Birkrigg
Dalton-in-Furness
BARROW-IN-FURNESS

Legend:

○ Extant Circles
× Vanished Circles

▰ Land over 610m; 2000 feet

▱ 305–610m; 1000–2000 feet

E.W. Ennerdale Water
L. Loweswater
C.W. Crummock Water
B. Buttermere

5   0   5   10 miles
5   0   5   10 km

Chapter Three

The Stone Circles of South and West Cumbria

Introduction

The locations of stone circles in Cumbria are shown in fig. 3.1. It can be seen that most are situated around the central dome of the fells, and very few are on land higher than 300 m. In the figure, the circles of the south and west are divided from those of the north and east. It is a somewhat arbitrary division: there is, for instance, no particular reason for drawing the line to the west of Castlerigg rather than to the east; but it is not completely without significance. Most of the circles in the south and west lie on the coastal plain or on nearby hills, whereas those of the north and east cluster along the Eden valley. Communication between the communities that used the southern and western circles would have been relatively easy both by land and round the coast by boat; therefore, one would expect to find similarities between the various types of circle in the south and west, as is indeed the case. The circles of the Eden valley region, however, are cut off from the west and south by the Cumbrian and Howgill Fells. In prehistoric times communication between west and east by a direct route must have been very arduous, as can be vividly experienced today during a drive over Hardknott and Wrynose Passes. The easiest route would have been a much longer one, via the Carlisle lowlands to the north.

This mutual isolation might be expected to have led to differences between stone circles in the two parts of the county. This is true to a certain extent. Large open stone circles of later neolithic date occur throughout Cumbria; examples include Swinside in the south-west, and Long Meg and her Daughters in the far north-east. This distribution is consistent with their use by scattered communities engaged in some long-distance activity, such as trade in stone axes (p. 7). The difference between the two parts of the county, however, becomes apparent when the smaller, sepulchral circles of early bronze age date are considered. These circles were probably for the sole use of small, local communities, in contrast to the earlier circles. In the north and east of Cumbria many of these sepulchral sites fall into the category of cairn-circles (fig. 2.1d). These consist of standing stones, often fairly large, set around the edge of a burial cairn; examples include Little Meg and Leacet Hill. There are no comparable sites in west and south Cumbria. Here, however, are several embanked circles (fig. 2.1e); these are described as a group towards the end of the chapter (p. 77).

Open stone circles (fig. 2.1a) are scattered throughout west and south Cumbria, with the exception of the southern coastal plain. The absence of open stone circles in this area led R. G. Collingwood to suggest that timber circles may have been built here to cater for ceremonial needs;[1] but there is certainly no evidence for this suggestion. It is more likely that either open stone circles were never built here, or if they were, they were destroyed before the existence was recorded. This last possibility is quite feasible. Good farming land has always been scarce in this part of Cumbria, and several open circles on the western coastal plain, such as Kirkstones and Annaside, have been destroyed within the last century or two for the benefit of agriculture. There are suggestions of even earlier destructions, such as that of the possible circle of Le Wheles, near Whitehaven.

A third distinctive class of stone circle in the west and south of the county consists of a free-standing ring of large stones surrounding a smaller burial mound or cairn (fig. 2.1a). The circles on Burnmoor are of this class, and Clare has used the term 'Burnmoor-type' to describe this sort of circle.[2] Other examples in the region are Grey Croft and Blakeley Raise.

It is worth repeating an earlier caution (p. 13). Present-day appearances may be deceptive: two circles of apparently similar type may not have close chronological or cultural connections.

The geology and landforms of the region are both very varied. The central fells are composed of three main types of rock, which tend in broad bands from west-south-west to east-north-east southern fells are of Silurian shales, and the northern fells of Skiddaw slates and related rocks. Between the two are rocks of the Borrowdale Volcanic series. The lower land around the fells is of younger rock. To the north, the fells are bounded by Carboniferous limestone, which forms low hills before giving way to the Carlisle plain. This area of low lying ground is mainly of Triassic rocks (sandstones and mudstones), but it is covered widely by thick glacial deposits, which in places are raised up into drumlins. The area of low land narrows considerably in the west between the fells and the sea. Between Maryport and St Bees Head the rocks of the coastal plain and the low hills to the east are formed from the coal measures (mainly sandstones). A strip of Carboniferous limestone, narrower than in the north, separates these rocks from the older rocks of the fells. South of St Bees Head, the coastal plain narrows even further. The coal measures and Carboniferous limestone give way to Triassic sandstone, which forms a band of low-lying, cultivated land between the sea and the fells. The Carboniferous limestone reappears across the Duddon estuary, and it borders the northern part of Morecambe Bay. The line of the limestone is broken by the estuaries of the Leven and the Kent, and here the older Silurian rocks are exposed. The outcrop of limestone continues eastward to the Lancashire border.

Druids' Circle

Location: SD 292739
On Birkrigg Common 5 km
(3 miles) S of Ulverston
70 m above sea level

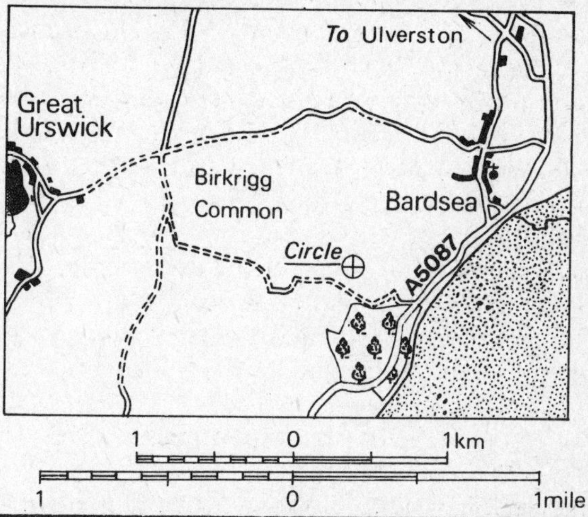

There is a noticeable change in scenery to the south of the market town of Ulverston. Here the light-coloured Carboniferous limestone contrasts vividly with the older, darker rocks to the north. An immediate indication of the change of geology is the white drystone walling of the area. The limestone forms a region of low hills, rising to heights of 100 m or so, and often capped by a bare exposure of limestone. Birkrigg Common is the highest of these hills. It lies 5 km (3 miles) south of Ulverston midway between the villages of Bardsea and Great Urswick, and it rises gently from the coast to a height of 136 m. The lower slopes are thickly covered by bracken; but many short-turved paths and trackways, used by sheep and afternoon strollers alike, criss-cross the common and manage to keep bracken-free. A heavily eroded, bare limestone pavement appears towards the top of the common.

There is much evidence of prehistoric occupation on and around Birkrigg. Several bronze age tumuli are to be found on the common, although many of them are rather indistinct. Around the summit of Skelmore Heads, the next hill to the north-west, is a prehistoric enclosure and a long cairn.[3] In a field about 0.5 km (⅓ mile) to the west of Urswick Tarn are the possible remains of a megalithic chambered tomb. 'Urswick Stone Walls', a short distance to the north-west of Little Urswick, is a site consisting of enclosures and hut-circles of just pre-Roman date.[4]

The Druids' Circle (see plate 1) lies on the south-east side of Birkrigg Common, about 0.5 km from the coast. To the north-east it overlooks the village of Bardsea, with its white-walled church; and to the south-east the sands of Morecambe Bay stretch into the distance. A relatively flat area of land, on a slope that rises gently to the north-west, was chosen for the site of the circle. The site is very easy to visit. A minor road leaves the A5078 2 km (1¼ miles) south of Bardsea and goes over Birkrigg Common. It passes close to the circle, which can be reached by walking along one of the short-turfed pathways. Its ease of access means that it has not

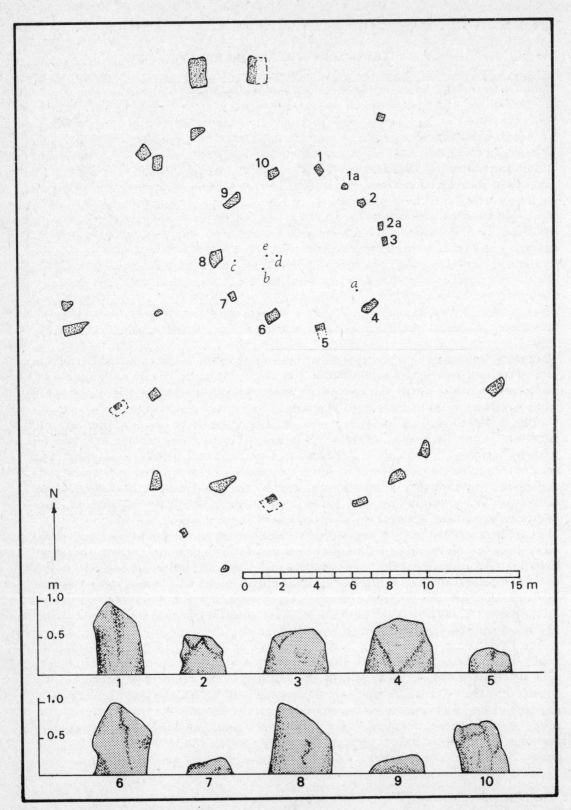

Fig. 3.2 The Druids' Circle, Birkrigg.

escaped the attentions of owners of spray-paint cans (who leave their modern graffiti on the ancient stones) and metal-detectors; the users of the latter, however, are doomed to disappointment, for there are no riches to be found here.

The Druids' Circle consists of two roughly concentric stone rings. This makes it fairly unusual, as only thirty or so concentric stone circles are known in Great Britain (p. 14); the best known example is Stonehenge. Only one other, Kirkstones, is known from south Cumbria, but this has been completely destroyed.

The inner ring has a diameter of 8.5 m. Inside this the ground is free from the encircling bracken and is covered by short turf. A number of depressions are visible in the ground here; these probably result from the excavation of the circle. The 12 stones of the inner ring are of the local Carboniferous limestone, and it may be that the outcrop of limestone a few metres to the north of the circle was the source of the stones. The stones have all been heavily weathered with the deepest pitting on their south and south-west sides, i.e. on the sides facing the prevailing winds. Stone 6 has been sculptured into a shape resembling the head of a sperm whale, mouth ajar, rising out of the sea. All the stones lean towards the centre of the circle; and apart from stones 1a and 2a, which just protrude through the turf, their vertical heights vary from 0.3 to 0.95 m. The tallest stones are in the north (no. 1) and the south-west (nos. 6 and 8). It may be significant that stones 4 to 9 alternate in height. The regular shapes of the stones, especially nos. 1, 2 and 6, may indicate that they were dressed before being set in position.

The outer ring consists of about 20 stones placed very irregularly, and has a diameter of about 24 m. It is much less conspicuous than the inner ring, and many of its stones are low and obscured by bracken. Large portions of several stones are also covered by turf. The extent of some of the stones below the turf was determined by probing, and this is shown in fig. 3.2 by broken lines. A problem in surveying the outer circle is the large number of spurious stones showing above the turf; it is difficult to know which of these are meant to be part of the circle. There is a wide gap in the north-east, and probing did not locate any buried stones here. If the outer ring had been completed in this sector, the stones have since disappeared.

Excavation of the site was carried out in two stages by the North Lonsdale Field Club: in 1911 they examined the inner circle,[5] and 10 years later they tackled the area between the inner and outer circles.[6] The results show that early bronze age people buried the cremated remains of their dead here; and there was some indirect evidence that the site was used for ceremonial purposes as well. On removing the turf from inside the inner ring, the excavators found a pavement of cobbles a few centimetres below the surface, extending to the outer ring. The cobbles were not local limestone, as might be expected, but were 'blue rag'; so the builders had taken some trouble to obtain them. Beneath these cobbles, a second pavement was discovered, but this was not as extensive as the upper one. The remains of the cremated burials were found below the lower layer of cobbles at points *a*, *b*, *c* and *d* (fig. 3.2). At point *a*, a large undressed stone in the lower pavement covered fragments of calcined bones, which lay on a third layer of cobbles. Nearby were the two halves of a disc of fine sandstone, the edges of which had been sharpened as if it were a tool. The interments at points *b*, *c* and *d* consisted of calcined bones and charcoal at the bottom of shallow pits. The cremations may have taken place above the specially-dug pits, and the remains allowed to fall to the bottom. The most significant find was at point *e*, very close to the pit at *d*. Here, 50 cm below the lower pavement, a collared urn of early bronze age date was found inverted over black earthy material, charcoal and calcined bones; it was unfortunately broken during excavation. The urn is reddish-brown and made of a mixture of fine and coarse grits. When reconstructed, it had a height of 13.4 cm and a diameter across the rim of 12.6 cm.[7] It had been decorated on the outside by a lattice of twisted cord (fig. 3.26a). It is not possible to date the urn precisely, but it may well have been made around 2000-1800BC. A similar urn was found in a tumulus not far from the Druids' Circle.[8] This tumulus also contained burial pits like those in the Druids' Circle.

The later excavation of the area between the inner and outer rings produced no evidence of interments, but three of the objects discovered may have been used for ceremonial purposes. A pear-shaped piece of stone, 15 cm long, was thought to be a pestle for grinding pigments; and near to this was an oyster-shaped stone with a handle on one side, and a circular depression carefully flaked out of the centre; this may have been a palette for colours. The third object was a piece of red ochre, possibly used for pigment. Other finds included several shaped and sharpened flakes of stone, which may have been implements. Stone 1a of the inner ring was also found during the excavation, buried between stones 1 and 2; its top was left showing above the turf after the ground was made up.

Do the results of the excavations allow us to answer the basic questions: when was the circle built and for what purpose? The cinerary urn can be dated to the early bronze age, and the burials tell us of the sepulchral nature of the circle; but it can hardly have been used as a cemetery, even a family one, for there are only five burials here. Other, unanswered, questions arise. Why are there three different types of interment? Does this imply that the site was used for a prolonged period during which rituals changed? And what was the purpose of the layers of cobbles? Were they placed there to seal the burials beneath? Similar pavements are known at other circles in the north-west of England, e.g. Bleaberry Haws (p. 41) and Mosley Height;[9] and Stonehenge has a layer of bluestone chips, which may be comparable. Also, what is the relationship between the circle and the other burial sites on Birkrigg Common? As mentioned earlier, similar burials and urns have been found in nearby tumuli. In some ways the Druids' Circle is like a tumulus that has not been covered by a mound. In fact, a burial mound 600 m west-north-west of the Druids' Circle covers a circle of stones 4 m in diameter surrounding many circular patches where fragments of cremations appear to have been placed. The stones are about 60 cm long and, like the stones of the Druids' Circle, they incline inwards.[8]

What we cannot hope to recreate are the beliefs of the circle builders and the ceremonies they carried out here; the bare bones of the finds do not help us. The imagination easily conjures up visions of painted figures, illuminated by the light of the funeral pyre, dancing in their sacred circle. But this is pure speculation. Whatever beliefs these people had died with them. Yet standing alone in this circle of ancient weathered stones, looking down to the sea and hearing only the song of the soaring lark, it is easy to think that some of their magic still remains.

Bleaberry Haws

Location: SD 264946
2 km (1¼ miles) WNW of
Torver on Bleaberry Haws
320 m above sea-level

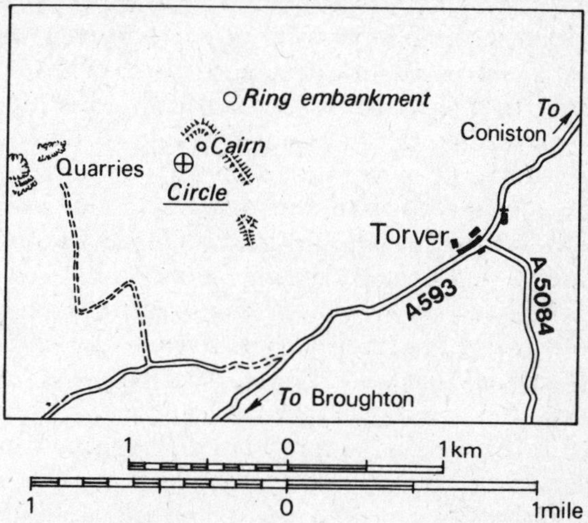

[map showing: Ring embankment, Cairn, Circle, Quarries, Torver, To Coniston, To Broughton, A593, A5084; scale 1 0 1km, 1 0 1mile]

The easiest approach to this tiny stone circle is from the quarry road shown on the map. Leave the quarry road at the point where it turns sharp left, and cross a drystone wall. Walk due north up the hill until the crest of the hill is reached. The circle is found by following the crest in a north-westerly direction. There may be some difficulty in locating the circle, owing to its small size and the low elevation of the stones; but a conspicuous cairn on top of a hill 200 m to the north-east of the circle is a good marker. The land beyond the quarry road is generally marshy, and at certain times can be very wet indeed; however, the drainage improves as the land rises, and the land in the vicinity of the circle is quite dry.

The circle is built on locally level ground on a ridge that slopes gently upwards to the east-north-east. The land falls steeply away to the north-west down to a shallow valley several metres below the circle. Tufted grass grows over the whole area and supports the usual population of sheep. The Old Man of Cóniston and Dow Crag dominate the view to the north and north-west; the Duddon estuary can be seen opening out to the sea, far to the south-west; and a short distance to the west are the blasted outlines of a quarry that produces the local green slate – the best slate in the world, according to the Lakeland antiquarian, W. G. Collingwood.

The seven stones of the ring form an ellipse of axes measuring 4.7 m and 3.7 m between the inner faces of the stones. It is the smallest free-standing stone circle in the region; and its small size and shape suggest it may be one of the most recent (p. 27 and fig. 2.9). Stone 5 has a large portion of its upper surface buried beneath the turf, suggesting that it has fallen outwards. The extent of the buried portion, as shown in fig. 3.3, was determined by probing. All the stone appear to be composed of the local Silurian shale. There are many similar stones within sight of the circle; so it seems that the builders did not have far to look for their material.

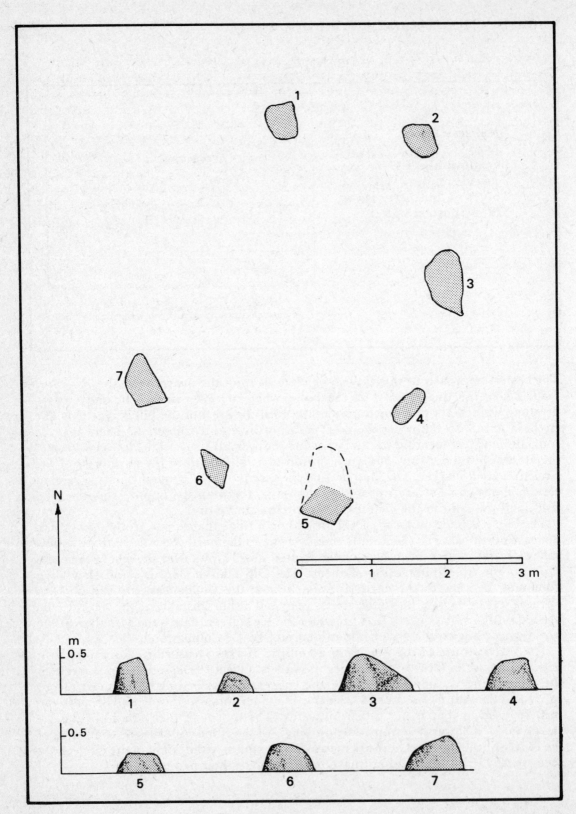

Fig. 3.3 Bleaberry Haws.

A cursory excavation was carried out at the end of the 19th century by Mr. H. S. Cowper.[10, 11] The arrangements for the excavation seem to have been rather lax, as the circle was dug into in the absence of Mr. Cowper. A rough pavement of cobble-stones was found, 60-90 cm below the surface, resting on the natural rock. Neither the extent of the excavation nor the presence of any other finds was mentioned in the brief report; therefore any suggestion for the use of the circle can only be speculative. The pavement of cobbles, however, suggests a link with the Druids' Circle on Birkrigg, in which cremated interments were found; moreover, a late date for the Bleaberry Haws circle also suggests that it would have been used for sepulchral purposes. It may not be unreasonable, therefore, to infer that this small circle was built towards the end of the early bronze age by a small group of people, perhaps a single family, as a place of burial.

The surrounding countryside is comparatively rich in prehistoric remains. Their are several cairns on Bleaberry Haws, some of which have been found to hold bronze age burials,[10] and a dyke of unknown antiquity runs from north-west to south-east about 250 m east of the circle. Four hundred metres to the north-east of the circle is a ring-embankment consisting of a roughly circular bank of earth and small stones. The low bank, about 3 m wide and less than 1 m high, surrounds an area 14 m in diameter.

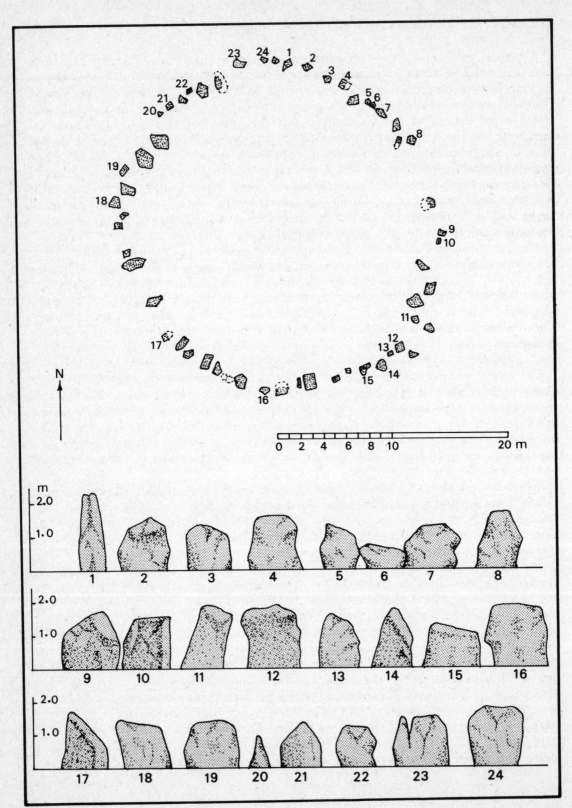

Fig. 3.4 Swinside, after Dymond.[14]

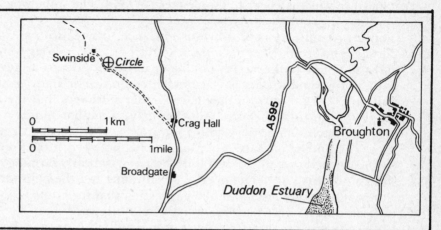

Swinside

Location: SD 172883
Near Swinside Farm
4 km (2½ miles) W of
Broughton
220 m above sea level

This splendid circle, described by Burl as 'the loveliest of all the circles'[12] can be compared only to Castlerigg and Long Meg and her Daughters in its visual impact; but its charm – for great charm it undoubtedly has – is greater even than theirs.

The circle is easily found; in fact there is a signpost pointing the way off the A595 along a minor road via Broadgate. At Crag Hall the visitor must take to his feet and walk along a rough track for 2¼ km (1¼ miles). The circle lies to the right of the track just south of Swinside Farm, which has given its name to its far older neighbour. The circle is also known as Sunkenkirk, a name having its origin in a legend that the Devil caused the stones, which were being used for building a church, to sink into the ground at night.

Swinside (see plates 2, 3 and 4) now occupies an ancient meadow. It was built on locally level ground, on a valley side which slopes down to the south and east. The site is sheltered by high ground to the north and west, while to the south-east the land opens out to the Duddon Sands below. Far to the north-east, the craggy summits of the Dunnerdale Fells are visible.

The 51 remaining stones are set in a bed of rammed stones, and they form an almost perfect circle of diameter 28.7 m. The stones are very close together, in some places almost touching, and this gives the effect of an almost continuous wall of stone – one of the features of the earliest circles (p. 27 and fig. 2.9). Stones would have originally filled the present gaps in the east and south-west, and evidence of their former presence was found when the site was excavated.[13] Strangely, all the stones that have fallen have done so inwards. An explanation advanced for this is that sheep have sheltered in the lee of the stones; the hollows worn by their feet filled with water, and the resulting softening of the ground caused the stones to collapse.[13] It is not clear why sheep should select the inner faces; maybe they, too, were attracted by the mystery of the ring of stones! The stones are of local metamorphic slate known as 'grey cobbles'. The tallest (no. 1), a slender pillar 2.29 m high, is almost due north of the centre; and another tall stone, no. 9 (1.95 m), is diametrically opposite. Stone no. 16 has a deep vertical crack – evidence of a recent battle between it and a rowan bush over the same piece of land. The stone won a Pyrrhic victory: the bush is gone, but the great scar remains.

In the south-east is an obvious entrance, where two extra-circular stones form portals. The arrangement is similar to the entrance of Long Meg and her Daughters, and also to that of the circle of Ballynoe in County Down, a short boat-trip across the Irish Sea. Several writers have commented on the similarities between Swinside and Ballynoe;[15, 16] not only do they have similar entrances, but the tallest stones of both are in the north and south, and they have a similar number of stones set closely together. Such similarities surely indicate close contacts between the builders of both sites. The finding of many 'Cumbrian-style' polished stone axes in Northern Ireland (p. 7) also supports the idea of links between the early farming communities on both sides of the Irish Sea. The porch-like entrance and the palisade-like arrangement of stones at Swinside has led to the suggestion that the circle is a version in stone of an earlier wooden construction, perhaps built elsewhere.[2]

The site was excavated in the spring of 1901;[13] but, as is the case for many of the other large stone circles, little or nothing was found to help us understand its origins or its use. As mentioned before, the holes that formerly contained stones were found in the gap in the east. There was little suggestion that the site had been artificially levelled. The only finds to come from inside the ring were a piece of charcoal and minute splinters of bone from near the centre, and two pieces of red iron-stone, possibly used for pigment. The small pieces of charcoal and bone can hardly be evidence of an interment. They may be part of a 'dedicatory offering'; but the excavators had a more prosaic explanation – they were probably the result of top-dressing. So, like other 'ceremonial' circles of the neolithic age, the stones of Swinside keep their secrets to themselves.

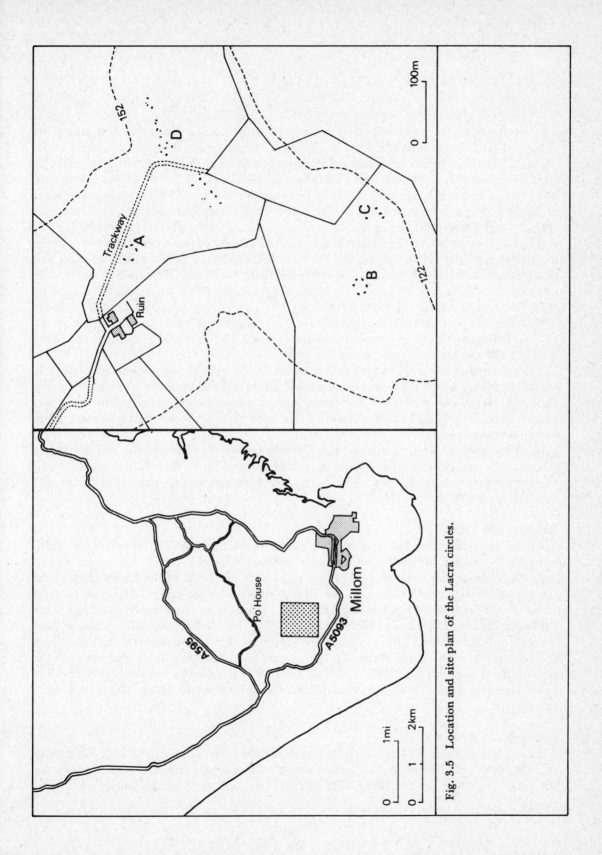

Fig. 3.5 Location and site plan of the Lacra circles.

The circles of Lacra were built high up on the south-facing slope of a hill above the village of Kirkstanton, to the west of Millom. The hill rises steeply from the coastal plain, which is only 2-3 km (about 1½ miles) wide here, to a height of 150 m. The sites of the circles overlook the Irish Sea and the Duddon Sands to the south and east; and to the north, across the valley of Whicham Beck, is the dark imposing mass of Black Combe. The name Lacra (or Lowcrow) belongs to the ruined farmhouse shown on the site plan (fig. 3.5).

The circles can be reached from Po House by walking along a trackway that climbs up and around the hill for about 1½ km (1 mile). The track is not a right-of-way, and permission to visit the sites must be obtained from Po House. The land on which the circles are built is very hummocky and covered by short turf. It is heavily grazed by cattle; but at some time in the past, more than a century ago, the land was under cultivation. It was this that probably led to the present ruinous condition of the circles; for many of the original stones would have been removed to allow the inner areas of the circles to be ploughed.

There are four separate megalithic remains in the group: two clearly recognisable stone circles (A and B), a much-delapidated circle (C), and a more complex site (D); they all stand on relatively flat terraces on the hillside. The whole site was investigated in 1947 by Dixon and Fell.[17] Circles B, C and D were partially excavated, but A was omitted.

Another megalithic monument, the Giant's Grave, lies just to the north-west of Kirkstanton, near the farm appropriately called Standing Stones. It consists of a pair of standing stones, 2 m and 3 m high, set 4 m apart. On the taller stone are cup-and-ring marks.

Lacra A SD 150813

This is probably the best-preserved circle of the group. It consists of eight irregularly-shaped, lichen-covered stones varying in height from 0.2 m to 1.0 m and set in a circle of diameter 15.7 m. The stones, like all those of the Lacra circles, are composed of rock that belongs to the Borrowdale Volcanic series. Evidence of their volcanic origin can be seen in the numerous vesicles in their surfaces. They were probably obtained locally; in fact, several similar boulders are visible within a short distance of the circle. The gaps in the circle in the south-western and northern sectors indicate that some of the original stones have been removed, and many of the remaining stones appear to have toppled. In 1874 it was reported that a stone had been recently removed from the circle, the circle itself being described as a hexagon![18].

Lacra B SD 149810

This circle lies some 350 m south of Lacra A down the slope of the hill. Six stones remain, although the excavation indicated that there were originally eleven. They are irregularly spaced and set in a circle of diameter 14.7 m. A small stone, no. 7, just

Fig. 3.6 Lacra A.

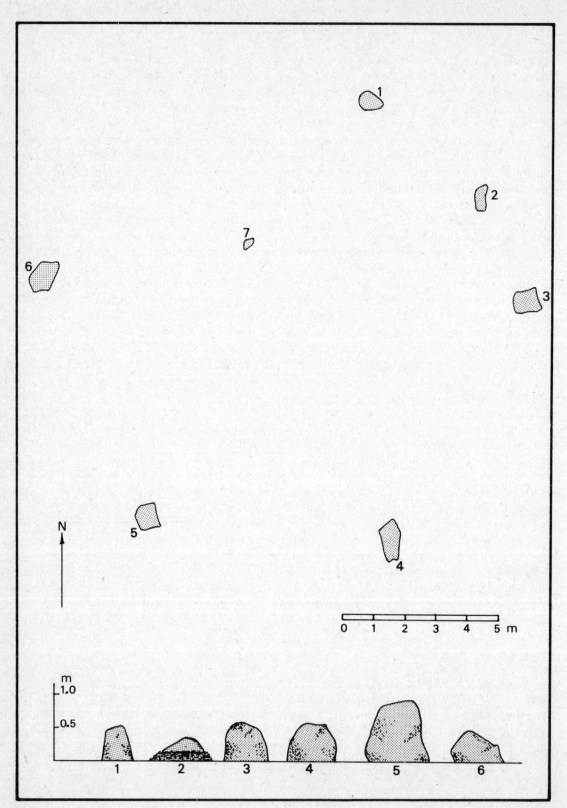

Fig. 3.7 Lacra B.

protrudes above the turf inside the circle. Apart from this inconspicuous stone, the inner area looks fairly featureless; but excavation showed that the original structure was complex. When the turf was removed, it was seen that a low mound of diameter 9 m, composed of earth and stones, had been constructed inside the circle. A flake of flint lay on top of the mound. In the north-east sector, also lying on top of the mound, was found part of a ring of stones, each about 60 cm long, set pointing towards the centre of the circle. Stone 7 may be a continuation of the ring farther to the west. If completed, this inner ring would have had a diameter of 4.8 m. A layer of earth, reddened by fire, was found near the centre of the mound just above the old turf-line; and much charcoal of ash-wood was also discovered here. Below the very centre of the mound, under some large stones, were found fragments of burnt bone – all that was left of the primary burial.

In size, the circle most closely resembles Lacra A; but as the latter has not been excavated, no further comparison can be drawn. It is interesting, however, to compare Lacra B with other stone circles in south Cumbria. The inner ring of stones, although buried, suggests similarities with the Druids' Circle on Birkrigg. Unlike this circle, though, no evidence was found for the use of either burial pits or cinerary urns. It is also worth recalling that a bronze age burial mound near the Druids' Circle covered a circle of similar size and structure to that of Lacra B. The 10-stone circle of Grey Croft also surrounds an early bronze age burial mound.

Lacra C SD 150810

A short distance to the west of Lacra B are the few stones that constitute the pathetic remnants of Lacra C. It may be difficult to visualise these stones as having formed part of a circle, but excavation has shown that they probably did. The largest stone (no. 1) has fallen outwards (as has no. 3), but it would originally have stood to a height of 1.5 m. The excavation of the site showed that at least stones 1 and 3 had been raised artificially, as their packing stones and socket holes were found. It was not ascertained whether stone 4 was part of the circle, but its position suggests that it might have been. The excavators found little else: an oyster shell lay close to the west side of stone 1, and a deposit of oak charcoal was found by stone 3. There was no trace of a central cairn or barrow. From the position of the stones, the original diameter was estimated to be about 24 m.

If the circle disappoints, the view on a clear day should not. Millom lies below to the south-east, between the hill and the shore of the Duddon estuary; and across the broad sands of the estuary are the shipyards of Barrow-in-Furness and the hills of Low Furness.

Lacra D SD 151813

Lacra D lies in a field known as Great Knott, 250 m east of the ruins of Lacra farmhouse. It is certainly the most complex and interesting of the four Lacra circles. Unfortunately, on the ground, the remains are difficult to interpret for two main reasons: the very ruinous condition of the monument, and the plethora of stones (which may or may not be part of the original structure) in and around the site. The

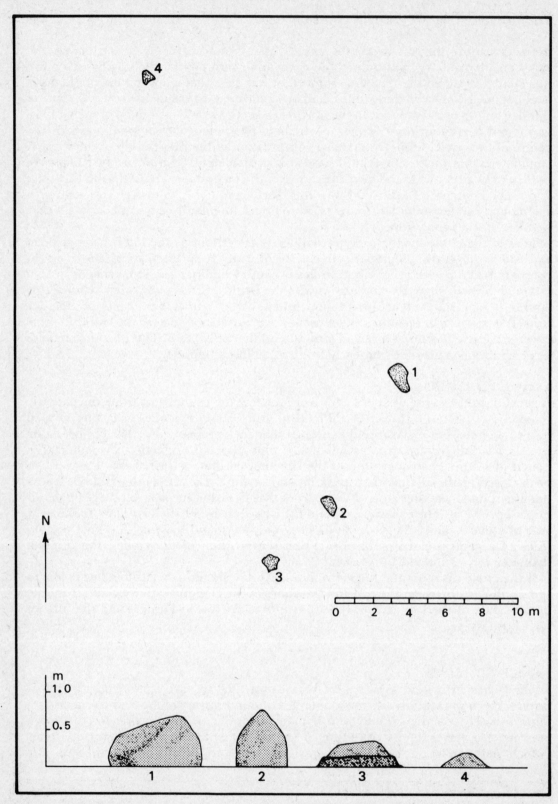

Fig. 3.8   Lacra C.

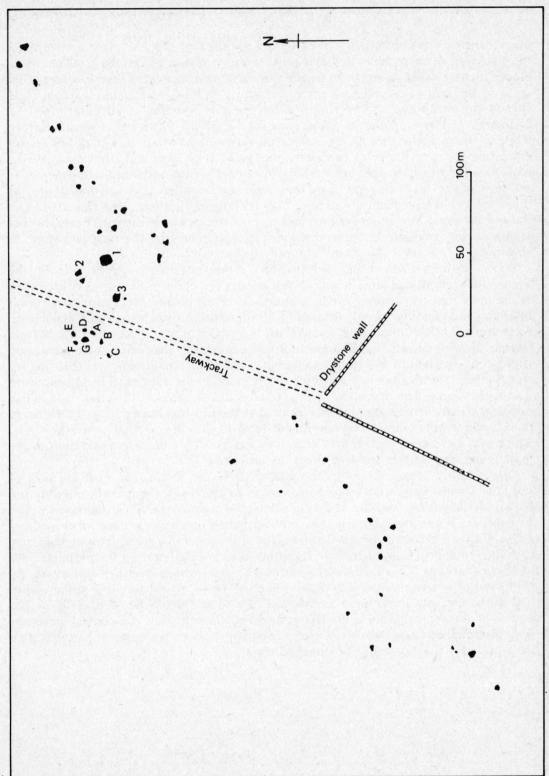

Fig. 3.9   Lacra D, after Dixon and Fell.[17]

main features, however, are more obvious on the site plan (fig. 3.9). Just to the east of the trackway is the main ring, having six or seven stones of various sizes set in an ellipse measuring 18 m north to south and 15 m east to west. There is a large, flat stone in the centre; its sides are approximately 2 m long, and it stands 0.5 m high. Just to the south-east of the ring are the possible remains of an outer ring. An alignment of stones, some in pairs, runs for 47 m east-north-east from the circle, while in the opposite direction can be seen the remains of an avenue of low stones extending for over 100 m to the west-south-west; it is 15 m wide, but many of the stones on the northern side are missing. A curved setting of stones a few metres to the west of the main ring suggests that a second, smaller, ring was built here; its diameter would have been about 5 m. Like its larger neighbour, this ring also has a flat central stone, but it is very low, and just protrudes above the turf. Several other stones of this small circle are in danger of being covered by the turf; and stone E, shown clearly on the 1948 plan,[17] can only be located by probing.

What uses were made of this complex site can only be conjectured. Presumably the avenue had ceremonial significance, but it is not even certain that it was constructed at the same time as the main circle. The results of the partial excavation carried out by Dixon and Fell give us only limited insight into the activities that took place here. Near stone 2 of the main ring an inverted collared urn was discovered, its bottom broken off, with oak and hazel charcoal in and around it – the remains of a cremation (fig. 3.26b). By the urn was found half a hazel nut shell, which indicates that the urn was placed in the shallow hole in which it was found in the autumn. The urn is now in Barrow Museum. The discovery of the collared urn shows that the circle was in use during the early bronze age; but it may be that the urn was buried at some relatively late date in the life of the circle and had little to do with the original use of the circle, which may have been ceremonial as well as funerary. A complete excavation of the main circle may answer some of these uncertainties.

Several other stone circles in the British Isles are associated with avenues of standing stones. Cumbrian examples include Kemp Howe (Shap) and possibly the Kirk on Kirkby Moor and the Moor Divock circles. One of the finest examples in the British Isles is the awe-inspiring circle of Callanish on the west coast of the Isle of Lewis. Callanish consists of tall slender slabs of stone set in a circle 13 m in diameter, with the remains of four avenues of standing stones radiating from the perimeter. As at Lacra D, there is a suggestion of an outer circle, which is either almost totally destroyed or was never completed; and there is also a central standing stone within Callanish. Comparisons, however, should not be taken too far, especially in the matter of the central stones; for Dixon and Fell thought that the central stones of both the small and large circles of Lacra D had never been set upright, and that they were probably the capstones of vanished cists.

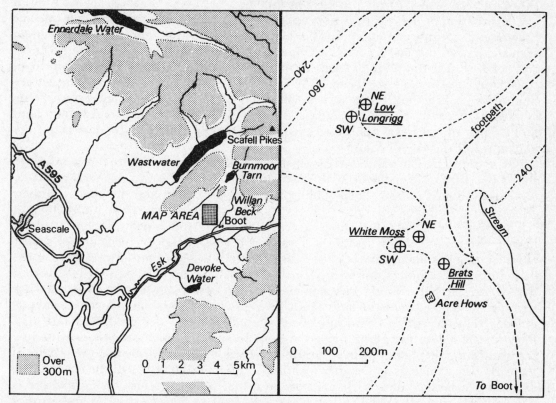

Fig. 3.10 Location and site plan of the Burnmoor circles.

North of the village of Boot in Eskdale is an area of moorland known as Burnmoor or Eskdale Moor. Amid the quiet of the moor are five stone circles: a single circle (Brat's Hill) and two pairs (White Moss NE and SW and Low Longrigg NE and south-west). The name Burnmoor apparently derives from 'borran', or cairn of stones, of which there are many in the vicinity of the circles.

The best way of reaching the circles is from Boot, but this requires a fairly strenuous climb up the side of the valley of Whillan Beck. The village of Boot is close to the terminus of the Ravensglass to Eskdale Railway, and in the summer it is a very popular spot for trippers; but on walking through the gate at the upper end of the village, the visitor is immediately greeted by the solitude of the moor. A footpath bears right from the gate and leads up the hill; to the right of the path is a stone wall, and beyond this the land falls down to Whillan Beck. Just over 0.5 km (¾ mile) beyond the gate are some ruined cottages once used by peat diggers. The way continues past the cottages directly up the hill. After a further 0.5 km (¾ mile) the first of the circles, Brat's Hill, is reached; the circle is just to the east of the rocky outcrop of Acre Hows, which serves as a good way-finder. From the Brat's Hill circle the pair of circles on White Moss are clearly visible 100 m to the north-west. The two

53

other circles are 0.5 km (¾ mile) to the north-north-west of Brat's Hill on the ridge of Low Longrigg, which forms the local skyline.

The situation of the circles is best appreciated from the more distant pair on Low Longrigg. From this vantage-point the circles of White Moss and Brat's Hill can be seen clearly, set out on the plateau below. The scenery is magnificent. To the north and north-west is the ridge of Illgill Head and Whin Rigg, dissected by a number of steep-sided stream valleys; beyond the valley of Whillan Beck to the north-east are fine views of Lingmell Crag and Scafell; and further round to the east are the mountains beyond Eskdale, including the craggy outline of Great Haw. The land drops down to the west, and between the fell sides is a vista to the coast and the mountains of the Isle of Man beyond.

Burnmoor is seldom visited; the occasional walkers may pass here on their way to Burnmoor Tarn or over the ridge to Wasdale Head. The visitor to the circles is likely to be noticed only by the sheep. The isolation of the circles and the beauty of their surroundings combine to endow the circles with an almost mystical quality.

The circles are 260-280 m above sea-level, and the land is peat-covered: wet and barren, the thin acid soil supports only coarse grasses fed on by flocks of sheep; however, this has not always been the case. There is evidence for farming here in the early bronze age; and as these early settlers probably built the circles, the dating of the farming activity should give some indication of the age of the circles. Before farming could take place, the land had to be cleared of its existing tree-cover, and it is unlikely that the circles could have been built before this occurred. Evidence that forest clearance on the moor started around 1600bc (1900-2000BC) is provided by the results of pollen analysis from Burnmoor Tarn.[19] This date, around the middle of the early bronze age, is in keeping with the architectural features of the circles. The reason for clearance and settlement on land that is now useless for agriculture is two-fold. The climate in the early bronze age seems to have been drier and warmer than it is at the present, making land at this height more hospitable; and there is evidence that the cultivated lower-lying ground was beginning to become exhausted at this time; this would have provided an incentive to exploit the higher land that had been previously ignored. The many cairns of stones in the vicinity of the circles could well have resulted from field-clearance rather than having a sepulchral use. Excavation of one of the cairns found no evidence for interment within.[20] Cairn-fields dating from the early bronze age are found in similar situations elsewhere in Cumbria (p. 8) and in other parts of the British Isles. A particularly well-known group is in north-east Yorkshire,[21] where they lie at heights of 180-300 m above sea-level on southerly facing slopes, which would provide the best conditions for cultivation.

A deterioration in the climate started near the end of the first millenium BC, perhaps as early as 1400BC. The cooler, wetter conditions ended the brief settlement on these now-barren moors. Increasingly damp conditions and the encroaching peat put a final end to the use of the Burnmoor circles, if changing fashion had not made them redundant earlier.

Having discussed the Burnmoor circles and their setting in general terms, it is now time to describe each circle in more detail.

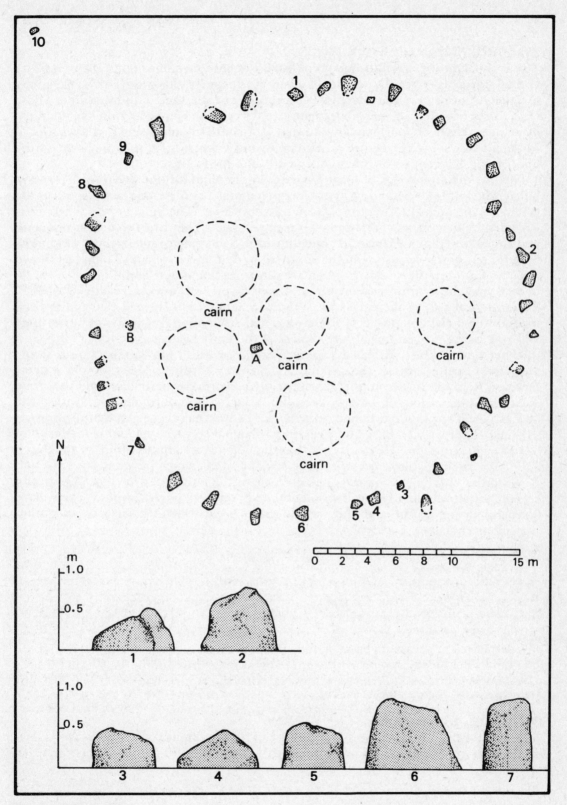

Fig. 3.11 Brat's Hill.

Brat's Hill (Burnmoor E) NY 176023
This is the largest of the Burnmoor circles. Forty or more stones set in the wet, peaty ground form an irregular circle of average diameter 30.4 m. There are many extraneous stones around the circle, especially outside the southern sector. These stones may have led an early investigator to describe the circle as being surrounded by an outer circle of 'fourteen large stones'.[22] An outlier, only 30 cm high, lies 27.1 m to the north-west of the centre of the circle; and interestingly, it is precisely on the line joining the centres of Brat's Hill and White Moss NE.

Most of the stones are of local Eskdale granite, and all but seven of them have fallen. The two tallest standing stones are just under 1 m high; one is due south of the centre (no. 6), and the other (no. 7) is in the south-west. The inner area of the circle is occupied by five cairns composed of stones and peat. They are 4 to 6 m in diameter and are hollowed in the centre. At one time each had a ring of small stones around its base.[23] Four of the cairns are in the southern half of the circle; and Thom has shown that the four outermost cairns lie on an ellipse having major and minor axes of 26 and 18 megalith yards respectively and a perimeter of 'almost exactly' 70 MY.[24] Excavation of two of the cairns by Wright in about 1826 showed that under each mound was a cist composed of five stones and containing fragments of burnt bone and stag horns.[22] Such burials are typical of the early bronze age.

Thom classes Brat's Hill as a Type A flattened circle;[24] the flattened arc is in the north-west sector, where the ground falls away downhill. Many of the stones, however, lie some way from the geometrically constructed perimeter; and the circle gives the impression of having been built in a haphazard fashion, with little observance of any predetermined plan (fig. 2.4). Clare has suggested that the present irregular shape was not based on a carefully-planned construction but is the result of a later reconstruction.[2] He points out that the bulging arc around stones 8 and 9 (fig. 3.11) may originally have been part of a smaller circle, which included stones A and B. A similar bulging arc on the opposite side of the circle may have been part of a second small circle. These two postulated smaller circles would each have surrounded one cairn, and they would have been similar in size to the other Burnmoor circles.

White Moss NE (Burnmoor D) NY 173024
The White Moss circles (see plate 5) share the same fairly level area of moorland as Brat's Hill, 260 m above sea-level. White Moss NE is the best preserved of the five Burnmoor circles. All its 11 stones are erect, and they form a perfect circle of diameter 16.2 m. The stones vary in height from 0.5 m to 1.1 m, and the tallest (no. 9) is due west of the centre of the circle. Occupying the central area is a cairn, measuring 5.5 m across its base, similar in appearance to those of Brat's Hill. There is no record of an excavation of this or of any of the cairns within the White Moss of Low Longrigg circles. It is obvious, however, that the mound has been despoiled, but its contents are unknown.

White Moss SW (Burnmoor C) NY 173240
This circle lies 46 m to the west-south-west of its neighbour. Like White Moss NE it is a perfect circle and has a similar diameter (16.6 m). It also contains a central cairn

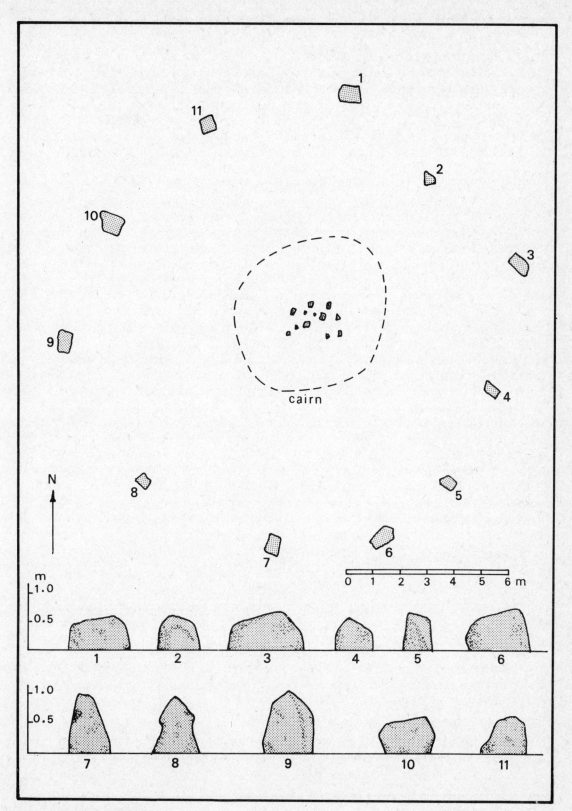

Fig. 3.12   White Moss NE.

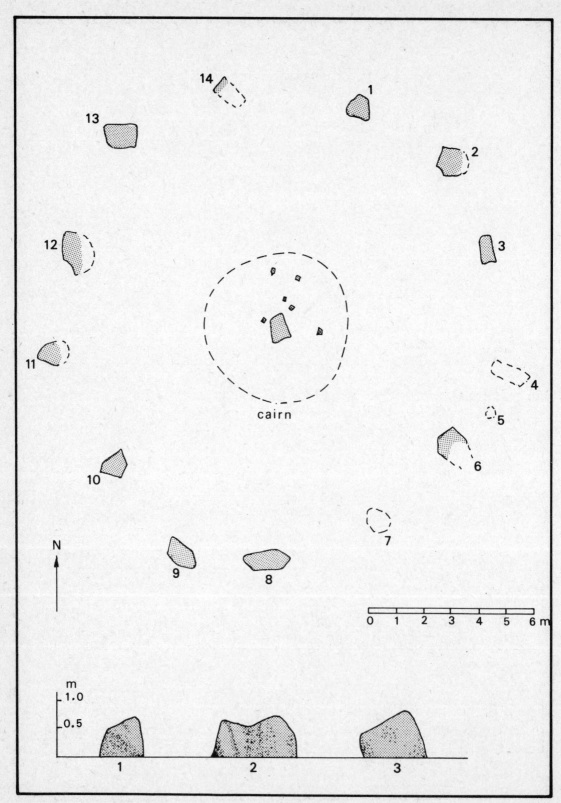

Fig. 3.13 White Moss SW.

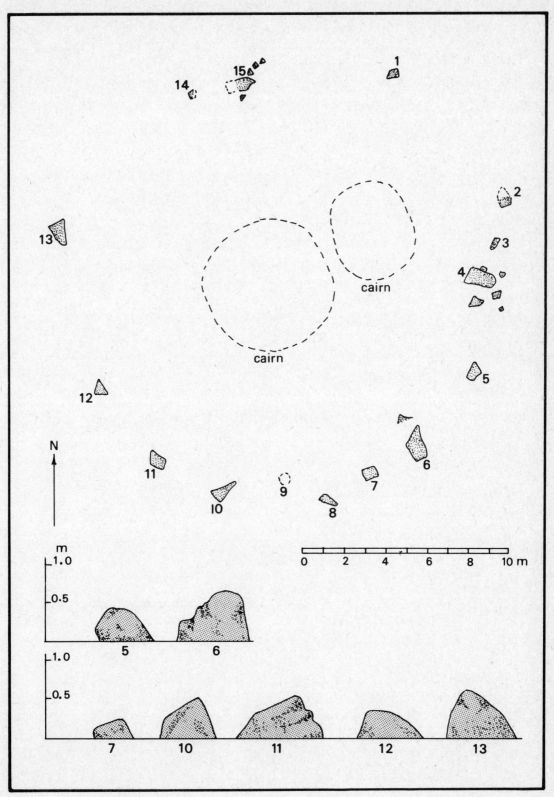

Fig. 3.14 Low Longrigg NE.

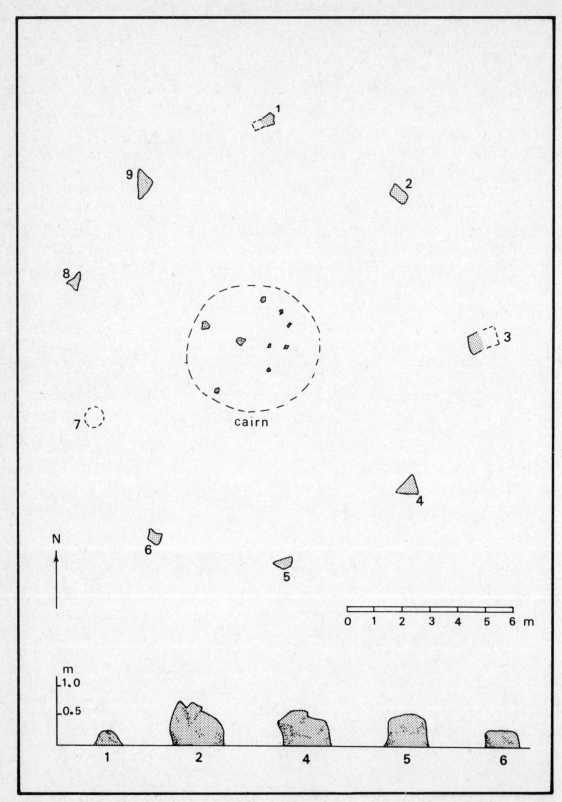

Fig. 3.15   Low Longrigg SW.

having a diameter of 5.2 m. It has, however, not survived as well. Of its 14 stones, only three (nos. 1, 2 and 3) appear to be still erect; many have fallen and are partly buried; and stones 5 and 7 are completely covered by the peat. The tallest of the erect stones, no. 3, is 0.8 m high.

Low Longrigg NE (Burnmoor A) NY 171028

The Low Longrigg circles are on the crest of a tongue of elevated land that slopes south-westwards from Boat How, 1 km (⅝ mile) to the north-east of the circles. Low Longrigg NE is a ruinous ring measuring 21.7 m from north-east to south-west and 20.4 m from north-west to south-east. It surrounds two stony cairns: the central cairn has a diameter of 6 m and the smaller one to the east of this a diameter of 4 m. The stones of the circle are low and tumbled. The tallest reaches a height of only 0.64 m, and stone no. 9 is completely buried. At two positions on the circumference, by stones 4 and 15, are complex arrangements of smaller stones, which lie higgledy-piggledy around the two main circle stones.

Low Longrigg SW (Burnmoor B) NY 171027

At a distance of 35 m across the boggy ground to the south-west of Low Longrigg NE lies the last of the Burnmoor circles. It is a true circle, 15.2 m in diameter, and it surrounds a single cairn 4.8 m in diameter. This is probably the wettest of the Burnmoor sites, and stone no. 4 is often surrounded by standing water. Like those of its companion, its stones are fairly low and mainly tumbled, although the highest stone, no. 2 (0.73 m), is still upright.

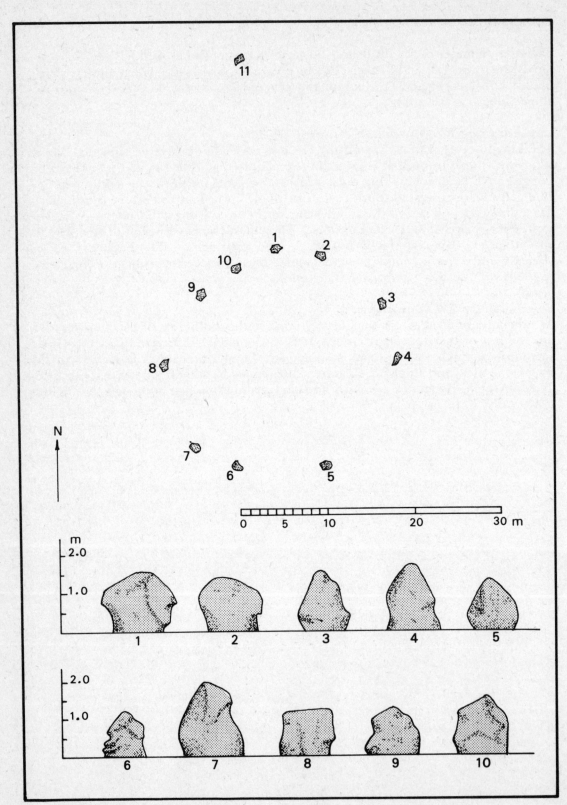

Fig. 3.16 Grey Croft, after Fletcher.[26]

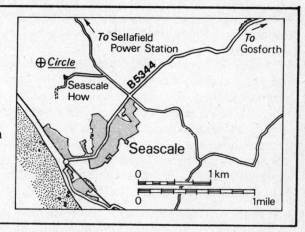

Grey Croft

Location: NY 033024
Near Seascale How Farm
3.5 km (2¼ miles) WSW Gosforth
25 m above sea-level

Few stone circles can have such an incongruous setting. It stands in a quiet pasture on a low crest of gentle slopes, with the Irish Sea only 0.5 km (¼ mile) to the west beyond the sand dunes. To the south and east the land dips down to a dry valley, with Seascale How farm on the crest beyond; and in the distance are the Lakeland Fells. To the north, however, is a vivid contrast. One km (½ mile) away, across a shallow valley, are the great cooling towers and buildings of Sellafield nuclear power station, a prosaic newcomer to an otherwise poetic scene.

The Grey Croft circle is reached by taking the road that leads to the nuclear power station from the Seascale to Gosforth road (B5344). A left turn off the former road leads to Seascale How farm, at which permission ought to be sought to visit the circle, which is 400 m north-west of the farm.

The stones of the circle are tall and impressive (see plates 6 and 7), reaching heights of just under 2 m. They are hard agglomerates of the Borrowdale Volcanic series, apart from no. 5, which is sandstone; and they were probably collected locally, as there are other similar glacial erratics in nearby walls and fields. Ten stones of the original 12 remain, and they are arranged in a flattened ring (Type D in Thom's system) having diameters of 27.2 m and 24.4 m. Almost due north of the centre is a low outlier at a distance of 34 m. When the circle was built, finding geographical north was not a straightforward task, because there was no prominent star near the celestial pole as there is today. North could have been located by determining south from solar observations at midday. An alternative method would have been to bisect the angle between the maximum eastern and western positions of a circumpolar star.

The circle has recently been reconstructed, following its destruction in the 19th century.[25] In 1820 the tenant farmer, James Fox, buried all but one of the stones (no. 1 in the plan) without permission of the landowner. Pits were dug by the stones, which were then toppled in. This 'improvement' was probably to aid ploughing. A highly-successful restoration was carried out in 1949 by Mr. W. Fletcher and the boys of Pelham House School, Calderbridge.[26] Some of the stones show signs of having been heavily battered – evidence of efforts to break them up.

The buried stones were located by probing, and many were found some considerable distance below the surface. The original exact positions of the stones were generally obvious from the packing stones that were still *in situ*. The bases of the stones were identified from the angles at which they lay; and their original orientations were estimated from the patterns of weathering on their surfaces caused by the prevailing wind. The locations of the two missing stones (between nos. 7 and 8 and nos. 4 and 5) were also discovered. By the base of stone 4, one of the boys found a broken polished stone axe from one of the Cumbrian axe factories. Excavation of the central area revealed the remains of a burial cairn, an oval of stones measuring 7 m by 3 m. Its presence can still be detected in a slight doming around the centre of the circle. Under the stones of the cairn were discovered fragments of charcoal and calcined human bone. The charcoal suggests a funeral pyre. Nearby were also found some flint flakes, a flint scraper, and a broken jet ring of probable early bronze age date. The finds are in the Tullie House Museum, Carlisle.

It is interesting to speculate about the relationship between the burial cairn and its surrounding stone circle. Fletcher thought that the burial cairn and circle were contemporary, implying an early bronze age date for both; it was believed that the presence of the neolithic stone axe was coincidental. This implies a greater similarity to the early bronze age burial circles, such as those of Lacra, than to the open circles of neolithic date. R. G. Collingwood, ignorant of the sepulchral use of Grey Croft, included it in his list of 'great circles', i.e. early ceremonial circles probably connected with the axe trade (p. 23). The architecture of the stone ring and its location support this view. It is at the coastal end of the route from the fells down through Eskdale, and a possible grinding and polishing site has been found nearby at Kell Bank (p. 5). Other stone axes have been found in the vicinity of Grey Croft.[27] An early bronze age date would argue against this connection. It is possible, however, to give another interpretation for the history of the circle, one that reconciles all the factors. This is to suppose that the broken axe was deliberately placed at the foot of stone 4, perhaps as a dedicatory offering during the construction of the circle. As the axe is unlikely to be later than the end of the neolithic period (p. 9), this interpretation implies a date for Grey Croft more in keeping with the early, open circles. If this were correct, the circle would be older than the cairn it surrounds; an original ceremonial use would have been changed to a sepulchral use as fashions changed.

Other circles tell a similar story. The early stone circle of Ballynoe in Co. Antrim surrounds a later burial cairn; and the henge monument at Cairnpapple in Lothian has an even more varied history. At this site a class II henge surrounding a stone circle was raised in the early bronze age over a late neolithic cremation cemetery. The stone circle was removed by food vessel users, and the stones used in the construction of a burial cairn within the banks of the henge. This was not the end of the story. The cairn was later enlarged to hold burials in collared urns; and the site may have been used for burials as late as the iron age.[28]

Finally we come to the outlier: what possible use could it have served? It is only 1 m high and is hardly prominent enough for a direction-marker for a traveller to or from the circle. Thom has suggested an astronomical use; it is on an alignment from the centre of the circle to the setting point of Deneb in about 2300BC.[29] But the fact that the circle has been reconstructed must leave a certain doubt as to whether the stones are in precisely their original positions.

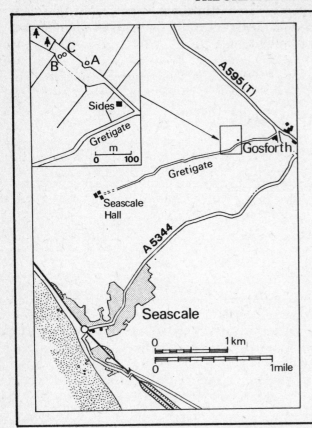

Gretigate

Location: NY 058037
1 km (½ mile) W of Gosforth
80 m above sea-level

It is strange that three stone circles could have remained unrecognised in an area so well investigated by 19th- and early 20th-century antiquaries. They were not identified until the late 1950s, by which time they were in a very ruinous condition. The largest of the three circles (Gretigate A) had suffered most. Like many stone circles on agricultural land, its presence was a hindrance to ploughing; so when the field in which it stood was first ploughed, in about 1900, many of its stones were dynamited and moved to the side of the field, where they now form indecorous piles.

The site of the circles is reached by leaving Gosforth along Gretigate, or 'gravel road', a rough trackway that leads to Seascale Hall. A narrow track leads off to the right about 0.5 km (⅓ mile) along, and this broadens out into a small field in which the two smaller circles (B and C) were discovered. The positions of the circles are shown on the site plan. The discovery of the circles was due to Mr. H. Stout, who also found several cairns in the small field in which circles B and C lie.[30]

Gretigate A

This circle had been built on a fairly level site on a sloping hillside. The only identifiable part remaining is a chord of the circle, about 30 m long, which has been incorporated into a stone wall along the edge of the field. Former stones of the circle, boulders of volcanic tuff and granite, have been deposited at the edge of the field nearby. The original diameter of the circle would have been about 32 m – quite an impressive size. The site has not been excavated, so it is not known whether it contained a burial, but there is now no obvious cairn or burial mound. Its estimated diameter and the comparatively large size of its tumbled stones suggest an early date for the circle, perhaps late neolithic, certainly earlier than the smaller circles B and C.

Gretigate B

Nine stones of an original number of 15 or 16 remained when Stout excavated this circle.[30] Six of the nine stones were still *in situ* and enclosed an irregular circular area of maximum diameter 21.9 m and minimum diameter 18.8 m. To the north-east of the centre was a layer of cobbles, probably the remains of a cairn. Patches of burnt earth were found inside the circle along with two holes containing carbonised wood, perhaps evidence of a cremation; but no other evidence of an interment was found apart from a worn tooth.

Gretigate C

This is the smallest circle of the group, with a diameter of 7.3 m. Nine of the original 12 stones remained when it was excavated. Like circle B, Gretigate C probably contained a cairn, as a cobbled area near the centre was found here as well; but little else of note was discovered. By one of the stones were two flint flakes, and by another were pieces of rounded haematite, which may have been used as a pigment. Among the cobbles were small deposits of carbon and an egg-shaped granite ball.

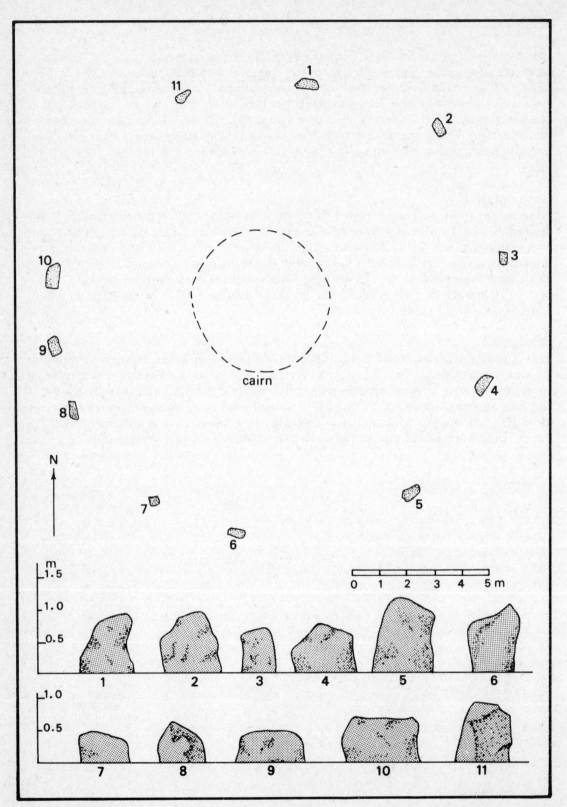

Fig. 3.17 Blakeley Raise.

Blakeley Raise

Location: NY 060140
On Blakeley Moss (Kinniside
Common)
4 km (2½ miles) W of
Cleator Moor
220 m above sea-level

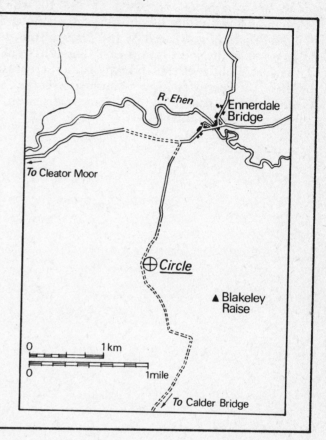

The fell road from Ennerdale Bridge to Calder Bridge passes within a few metres of this quietly impressive circle; for although it is fairly small (its diameter is 16.6 m), the stones are comparatively tall and are not obscured by surrounding vegetation.

The site of the circle is locally level, like that of so many of the other Cumbrian stone circles (see plate 8). To the east the land rises to the summit of Blakeley Raise (390 m). The ground falls away to the west to the valley of the charmingly-named Nannycatch Beck. Beyond the beck there is a clear view to the coast where the factory chimneys of Whitehaven are silhouetted against the sea; and far out across the Irish Sea is the Isle of Man. Round to the north, just showing above the local skyline, are the distant hills of Dumfries and Galloway, the most notable being the saddle shape of Screel Hill.

Blakeley Raise has been reconstructed, as evidenced by the concrete in which the feet of the stones are set. Reconstruction was carried out in 1925 by Dr. Quine of Frizington, but the accuracy of the rebuilding has been questioned.[2] It is reported that before the reconstruction the circle consisted of 13 stones, but eight of them had been taken away to make a gateway.[31] The circle now has 11 stones set in a perfect circle with a diameter, according to Thom, of exactly 20 megalithic yards.[32] The stones are of granite except nos. 2 and 10, which are of dark igneous rock. They surround a low tumulus of approximate diameter 5 m, in which there are two shallow hollows; there is no record of any finds within the mound. The tallest stone, no. 5 (1.15 m), is in the south-south-east. Thom has pointed out that the line joining stone 5, the centre of the circle, and the distant Screel Hill (azimuth 325°) gives the setting point of the moon at its maximum northerly setting during its 18.6-year cycle.[32] Owing to the uncertainty of the reconstruction, however, the significance of this alignment is questionable.

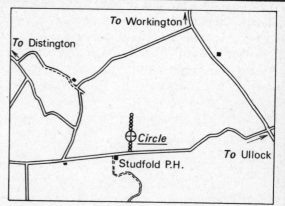

Studfold Gate

Location: NY 040223
On Dean Moor
8 km (5 miles) SE of Workington
190 m above sea-level

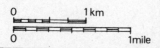

Dean Moor is an elevated tract of Carboniferous sandstone rising to heights of a little over 200 m. It lies to the south-east of Workington, and it is separated from the Lakeland Fells to the east by a broad valley occupied by the river Marron. The circle of Studfold Gate is on one of the highest points of the moor, 300 m north of the road from Ullock to Pica. On the 1:50,000 OS map the site is described as 'standing stones'. The location of the circle gives it a commanding view of the surrounding country. To the east are the fells; to the north the hills of Dumfries and Galloway form a backdrop to the Solway lowlands; and to the south the land falls gently to the coastal plain and the Irish Sea.

The circle is bisected by a stone wall, which, incidentally, forms part of the boundary between the districts of Allerdale and Copeland. On the west side of the wall, stumps of trees that once formed a plantation can be seen among the sedge grass; the field to the east of the wall is pasture. From the site of the circle, the land slopes down gently on all sides except to the north, where there is a gradual rise to the top of the hill.

The remaining stones of the circle are of the local sandstone, and they form one of the largest rings in Cumbria, measuring 25.9 m north to south and 32.8 m east to west. Considering the size of the ring, the stones are comparatively low and inconspicuous; several are totally or partially buried in the soft, wet earth, and others are probably not standing to their original heights. Climbing up to the site from the road, the visitor may well not notice the circle until almost reaching it. The tallest stone (no. 9) is 0.95 m high and has been incorporated into the wall, so has lost most of its visual impact. When erect, stone no. 1 may have been taller, as its longest dimension (determined by probing) is about 1.4 m. There are a number of large stones, which are not shown on the plan, just outside the northern arc of the circle. They are not set firmly in the ground, and give the impression of being an attempt at reconstruction, perhaps using stones from the wall.

An investigation and survey of the circle was carried out in the early 1920s by Mason and Valentine.[33] At that time the plantation to the west of the wall was

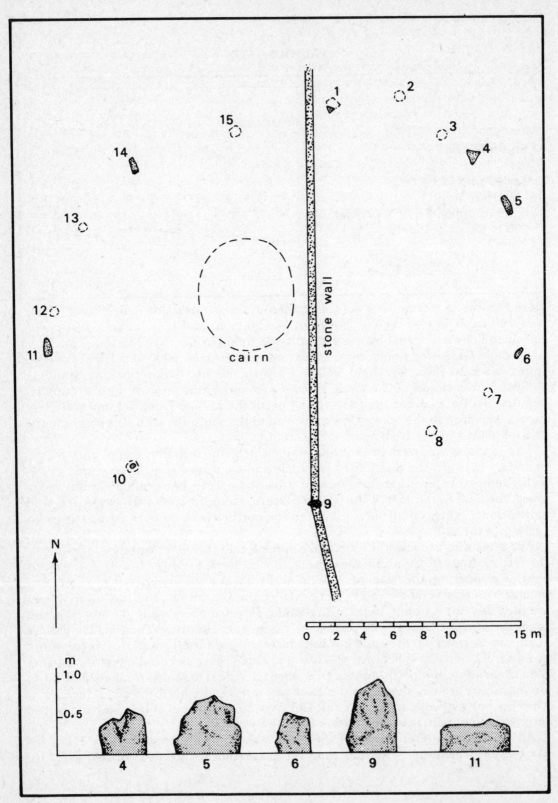

Fig. 3.18 Studfold Gate.

described as 'dense', and only one stone (no. 11) was found in this half of the circle; however, it was claimed that more stones had been visible in the plantation within living memory.[33] The trees have now gone, and five more possible members of this half of the circle can be located just above or below the surface. Stone no. 14 is 1 m long, and it is just visible among the long grass. These stones, however, may have been displaced from their original positions by activity in the plantation. The most noticeable feature in the western half of the circle is a low circular mound of diameter almost 7 m. It is composed of stones, many of which show through the cover of vegetation, and on its depressed top is a large stone slab. The mound is presumably the remains of a burial cairn, but a cursory excavation carried out by Mason and Valentine failed to provide definite evidence for this. Burl has pointed out that a burial mound is an unusual feature in a circle of this size,[34] and he has suggested that the mound was a later addition to the circle.[35]

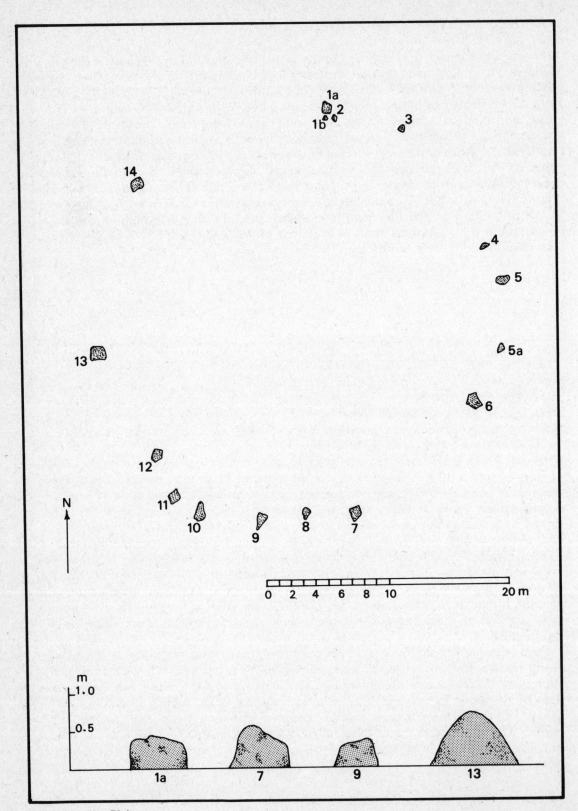

Fig. 3.19 Elva Plain.

Elva Plain

Location: NY 176317
Near Elva Plain Farm
5.5 km (3½ miles) E of
 Cockermouth
120 m above sea-level

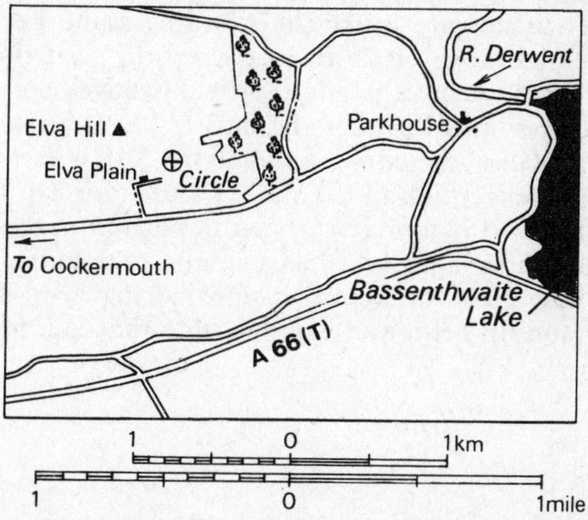

This circle lies on Elva Plain on the southern slopes of Elva Hill, which is the easternmost hill of an elongated stretch of highland tending east to west. From the site of the circle, the view to the east is dominated by Skiddaw across Bassenthwaite Lake, and to the south are the lower hills of Ling Fell and Sale Fell. Access to the site is from the minor road from Cockermouth to Barkhouse; and permission to visit the circle should be obtained from Elva Farm.

Situated on a level terrace on the hillside, the stones form an almost perfect circle of diameter 33.5 m. The interior shows no evidence of a burial mound or any other feature. It is one of Collingwood's great circles (p. 23), and as such is probably comparatively early in date, perhaps dating to later neolithic times. It has been linked with the trade in neolithic stone axes: the route from the factory sites in the central fells would have been along the side of Borrowdale and over the hills east of Bassenthwaite (fig. 2.8). The suggested association of the circle with the stone axe trade may find some support in the name of the site. Elva was rendered 'Elfhow' in records dating to 1488.[36] Although there are no reports of finds of stone axes in the vicinity, it may be that the name originates from the finding here of 'elfshot' – a term once applied to polished stone axes, which were thought to have some magic significance.

Even though the circle is a large one, the stones that compose it are mostly unimpressive; indeed, when the grass in the field has been cut, the positions of the stones are marked more obviously by the uncut tufts of grass that surround them than by the stone themselves. Fifteen stones remain of an original number of about thirty.[37] Of these, three (nos. 3, 4 and 5) are level with the ground, and one (no. 5a) is buried. The rest of the stones have fallen, with the possible exception of the tallest (no. 13), which stands to a height of 0.7 m at a point due west of the centre of the circle.

Anderson surveyed the circle in the early 1930s.[36] His plan shows an outlier 38° west of south of the circle at a distance of 55.4 m. There is now no trace of it in that position. The height of the outlier is not recorded; but it is unlikely to have been of any great height, unlike the standing stone Long Meg, which obviously points the way to its stone circle from the south; so if the Elva Plain outlier were used as a direction indicator, it would probably have been for showing the way from the circle. No astronomical use for the outlier has been suggested.

The plan of the circle shown in fig. 3.19 is essentially the same as that of Anderson, with the exception of the outlier and stone 1b. The latter is not seated firmly in the ground, and it may have been deposited here since Anderson surveyed the circle. Stone 7, although shown as a single stone in fig. 3.19, has five smaller stones around it. These have the appearance of having been dumped there, presumably from the surrounding field, and it is possible that one of them is the vanished outlier.

1. Druids' Circle, Birkrigg, from the west.

2. Swinside, view from the north-west.

3. Swinside, view through the entrance from the south-east.

4. Swinside, some stones in the northern sector.

5. White Moss NE from the east.

6. Grey Croft, view of the circle from the south.

7. Grey Croft, view across the circle from the east.

8. Blakeley Raise, from the west.

9. Castlerigg, looking south-west from stone 1.

10. Castlerigg, the entrance from the centre.

11. Castlerigg, the outlying stone by a fence, showing the plough marks.

12. Long Meg and her Daughters from the south.

13. The lowest set of carvings on Long Meg.

14. Spiral and concentric circles carved on stone 2 of Little Meg.

15. Broomrigg A, view of the circle from the east.

16. Shap Avenue, the Goggleby Stone.

17. Castlehowe Scar, view from the north.

18. White Hag, view from the north.

9. Gamelands, view from the north.

0. King Arthur's Round Table, the bank and ditch in the south.

21. Mayburgh, the standing stone from the east.

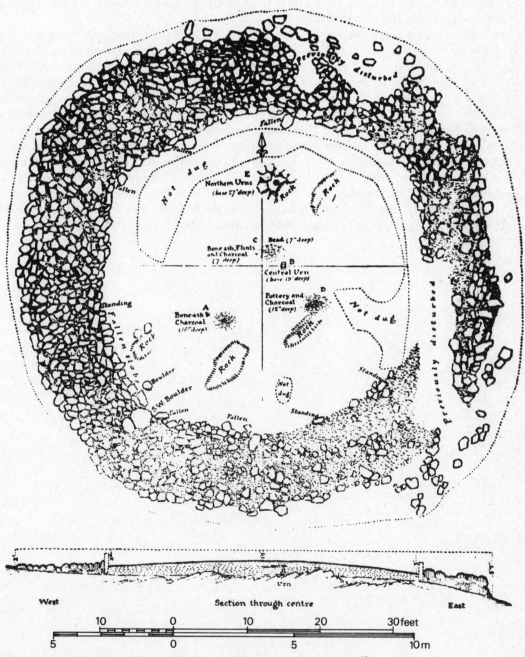

Fig. 3.20 The Banniside circle during excavation, after Collingwood.[40]

Embanked circles consist of an annular bank of earth and stones, with larger stones set into the bank, surrounding an inner area that is either fairly flat or slightly domed (fig. 2.1e). They are generally of low profile and unimpressive. Four such sites are described here: the Beacon near Lowick, the Kirk on Kirkby Moor, Banniside near Coniston, and the Casterton circle.

It is difficult to know exactly which sites to include in this category. There are several ring structures in south Cumbria that are so unimpressive as to be virtually invisible, or that consist of banks of earth or of small stones. It would be stretching the term 'stone circle' too far to include these, and they are best classed as ring-banks[38] or ring-embankments. An example of a structure of this type can be found on the top of Hare Crags, just to the north-west of Torver. An embankment 2 m wide forms a circle around the summit of the hill. No stones are visible in the bank, which appears to be composed entirely of earth. There is a suggestion of an entrance in the south-south-east, and traces of interment have been found within.[39] Also not included is the site in Levens Park, which bears a superficial resemblance to embanked circles, but which was found on excavation to have been originally a beaker dwelling (p. 9). The four embanked circles described here are either marked on the O.S. map as 'circle' or have been termed 'stone circles' by other authors.

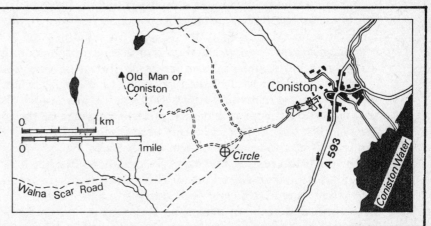

Banniside

Location: SD 286968
Near the Walna Scar Road
1.8 km (1⅛ miles) WSW of
 Coniston
245 m above sea-level

More is known about this circle than about the other embanked circles discussed in this section because it is the only one to have been systematically excavated; so it may give some clue to the nature of the other three. The Banniside circle lies below the imposing southern crags of the Old Man of Coniston just to the south of the Walna Scar Road, the old pack-horse route from Coniston to Dunnerdale. The circle is on a slightly raised bank, which slopes down gently from west to east. A short distance to the south the bank merges into marshy, low-lying ground, where there is a broad, reedy pool called Boo Tarn.

The present appearance of the circle is to some extent a product of the excavation. A low circular embankment of stones was originally faced on the inside by closely-fitting stone slabs. Most of these had fallen by the time the circle was excavated. The slabs in the south-west were re-erected and give a good impression of what the whole must have been like. Some of the slabs seem to have had their edges artificially straightened so as to increase the snugness of the fit and to give an almost horizontal ridge around the central area. Two tall slabs are also standing in the northern sector, the tallest being 60 cm high; and in the bank in the south-west is a large boulder about 1 m across. Stones are piled up on the outside of the slabs to form the bank, which varies in width from 3.7 m in the north to 3 m in the south, and it reaches its maximum height of 1.2 m in the east where the ground falls away. The inner area of the circle measures 14.6 m from north-east to south-west and 12.8 m from north-west to south-east. The centre of the circle is higher than the surrounding bank, but this rise in level is due mainly to back-filling after the excavation. The original profile is shown in fig. 3.20. It can be seen that although the central area was slightly domed, the centre did not rise above the level of the facing slabs.

The circle was excavated by W. G. Collingwood in 1909[40], and a plan of the excavation showing the positions of the finds is shown in fig. 3.20. The central area was found to have been artificially formed from a layer of yellow boulder clay placed on the bed-rock, and within this area several cremated interments were discovered.

The first to be located was just to the east of the centre at point B, where a crushed urn was found containing fragments of calcined bone and charcoal. It was thought that this was the primary burial on the site, and that the urn was broken when a later burial was inserted. The urn has been reconstructed and, like the other finds from the circle, it is now displayed in the Ruskin Museum in Coniston. Its appearance is that of a biconical urn – an unusual type in this part of the country – 20 cm high, 12.8 cm across its mouth, and 17.5 cm across its widest part.

Just to the north-west of the urn (point C) was a scatter of bone-ash and charcoal, among which were a small flint scraper and a bead of whitish-grey porcelain. It was this interment that may have caused the breakage of the biconical urn. At point D was another burnt spot, in which were discovered fragments of very coarse pottery thought to be the remains of two food vessels.

The most interesting discovery was made in the north of the circle at point E. A fine, almost intact collared urn, its lip unfortunately broken by the pick, was found in a hole beside an outcrop of rock. The urn measures 30.5 cm in height, 21 cm across its mouth, and 30.5 cm across its widest part. When found, it was half-filled with bone-ash, on the top of which was a pygmy urn containing the cremated remains of a child. Fragments of skull within the urn were thought to be those of a female; so it is tempting to think that the collared urn contained the remains of a mother and child. The most unusual object from the site was also found within the collared urn. Attached to a cinder was a fragment of finely-woven woollen cloth about 1.5 cm long. It has unfortunately not survived.

The pottery dates the circle to the early bronze age, and its use seems to have been largely, if not entirely, for burial. The same may well apply to the other embanked circles of the Kirk, the Beacon and Casterton. It is not possible to be more precise about the date of the Banniside circle from the results of the excavation, but its apparent similarity to the so-called enclosed cremation cemeteries of the Pennines may be useful in this respect. The site on Brown Edge, Totley Moor, to the south-west of Sheffield, yielded radiocarbon dates of 1530±150bc and 1250±150bc,[38] i.e. at the end of the early bronze age; and it is possible that these dates provide a guide to the age of the Banniside circle.

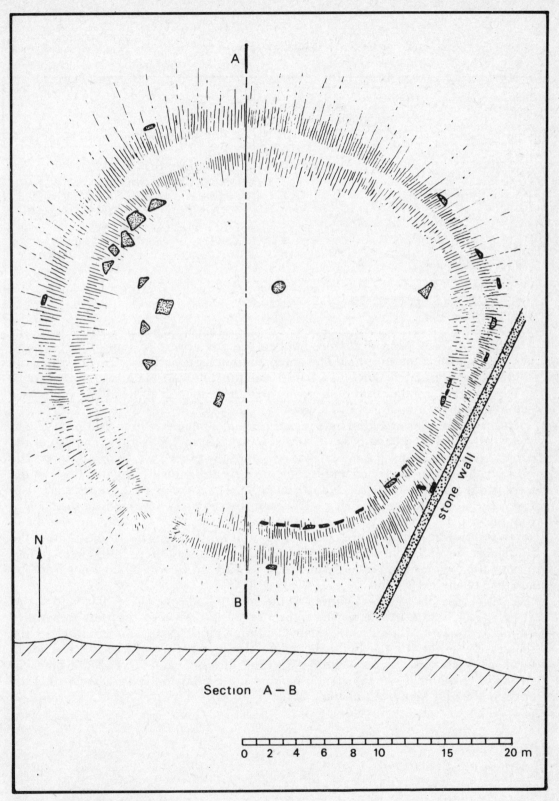

N

A

B

stone wall

Section A — B

0 2 4 6 8 10   15   20 m

Fig. 3.21 The Beacon circle.

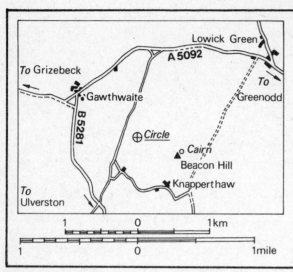

The Beacon

Location: SD 280842
Near Knapperthaw Farm, below
  Beacon Hill
3 km (2 miles) NW of Greenodd
135 m above sea-level

The Beacon circle is in a pasture-field to the south-west of Lowick Green, and permission to visit the site should be obtained from Knapperthaw Farm, to which the land belongs. The circle derives its name from the hill that rises just to the east of it. In former times, communication beacons were lit on the top of the hill, which is now featureless apart from a cairn of stones.

The circle consists of a level inner space varying in diameter from 26.1 m to 27.2 m and surrounded by a bank of earth and stones 2.5 m to 5.5 m wide. The top of the bank is generally about 0.4 m above the level of the inner area, but in the west the bank has been heavily eroded and is indistinct. As at Banniside, the inner face of the bank is lined with stone slabs, and in places slabs of stone mark the outer edge also. Five large stones, the tallest being 0.6 m high, are set on the inner side of the bank in the north-west. There is an entrance, which may be ancient, in the bank south-south-west of the centre, and a stone wall forms a tangent to the bank at the south-east. Several stones are visible within the circle, and those in the western half may be the remains of an inner structure. There are no records of any finds from the site, nor of any excavation.

A level rocky platform was chosen as the spot to build the circle. The land slopes gently down from south to north, and more steeply down in the west to a valley bottom below. As with so many other Cumbrian circles, one wonders whether the builders chose the site partly for the splendid views that it provides. To the north, Coniston Water can be seen fading into the distance, and beyond the bracken-covered Blawith Fells rise the greater heights of the Coniston Fells. Due north of the circle is the Old Man of Coniston.

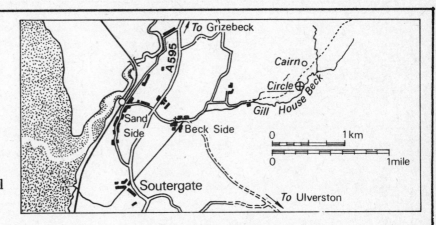

The Kirk

Location: SD 251827
On Kirby Moor, by
 Gill House Beck
5.5 km (3½ miles)
 NW of Ulverston
200 m above sea-level

This circle lies on Kirkby Moor, an area of elevated land in south Furness between the estuaries of the Duddon to the west and the Leven to the east. The best approach to the site is by an ill-defined path across the moor from Beck Side and Gill House. The path follows the northern side of the valley of Gill House Beck and passes close to the circle, which can be difficult to spot from a distance in the tall bracken of summer.

A roughly circular bank of earth and stone, varying from 5 m to 8 m in width, surrounds a relatively level inner area. The bank is about 0.3 m high, and in places its inner face is lined by larger slabs of stone set upright; the largest of these stones, 0.5 m high, is in the east. The outer boundary of the bank is indistinct and merges almost imperceptibly into the surrounding ground. Jopling, writing in 1846,[41] reported that large stones once stood in a line along the bank, but these had been removed several years previously for building material. The hollows still visible within the bank may mark the positions of these stones. The land on which the circle stands slopes down gently from north-east to south-west, but a few metres to the south-east the ground slopes down steeply to Gill House Beck.

To the north-east of the circle is an arrangement of standing stones, shown in fig. 3.22, which may be associated with the circle; however, it is not known for certain that they have been artificially erected. The stones are low, the tallest being only 0.65 m high, and they seem to form two intersecting avenues. One of the avenues tends to the north-east and is only about 1 m to 2 m wide, and the other, about 3 m wide, runs from north to south. There is another stone, not shown in fig. 3.22, 38 m to the north of the point where the two avenues intersect, and this may be a more distant member of the north-south avenue. It is interesting to note, although it may be of little significance, that the avenue leading to the north-east aligns with a notch on the hilly profile on the horizon (azimuth 51°). This is close to, if not at, the actual point where the sun would be seen to rise at the summer solstice.

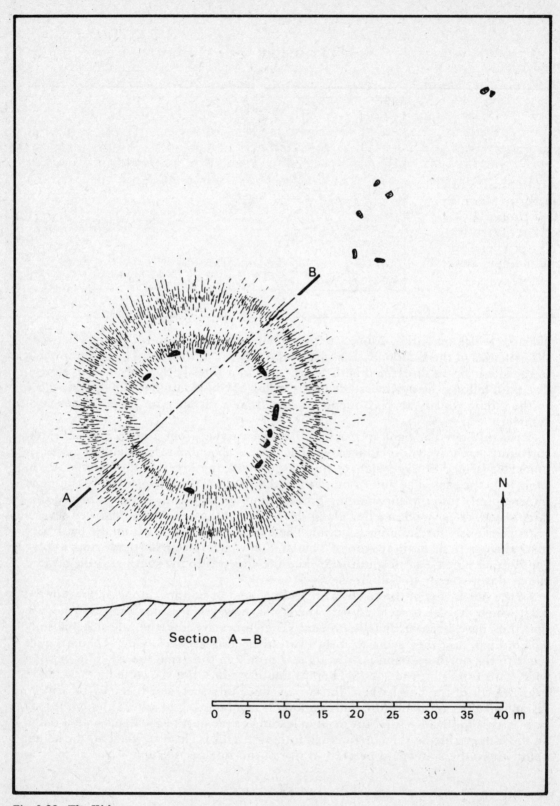

Section A—B

0   5   10   15   20   25   30   35   40 m

Fig. 3.22 The Kirk.

On higher land 315 m north-north-east of the circle, in a direction indicated by the north-south avenue, is a large cairn of cobble-stones. It measures 30 m across its base and is hollowed in the centre where it has been dug into. Within it were found a stone 'chest' and pieces of calcined bone.[41]

The Kirk has been used for social functions until comparatively recently. Well into the 19th century, the lord of the manor and his tenants congregated at the circle on Easter Monday afternoon. There they indulged in games of wrestling, dancing, hurling and leaping. Such pastimes were not without their dangers, and the last lord to attend broke his thigh during one of the games. Sober counsel prevailed, and the games were discontinued.

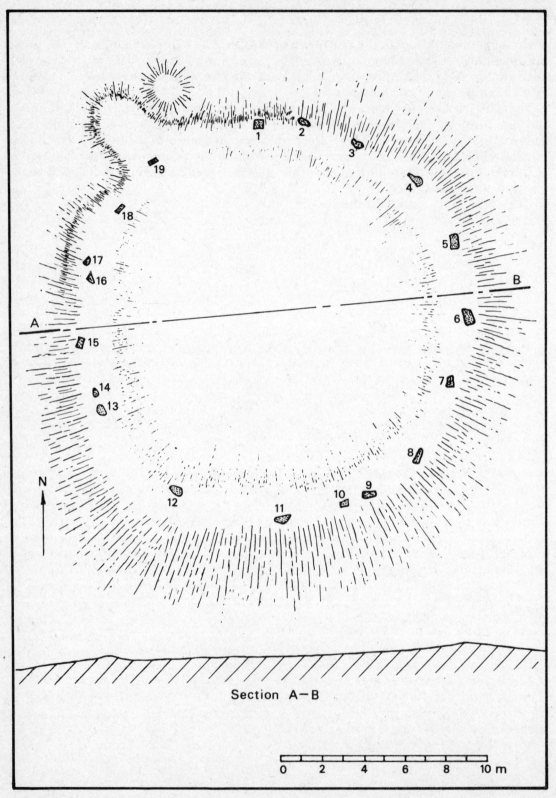

Section A—B

0 2 4 6 8 10 m

Fig. 3.23 Casterton.

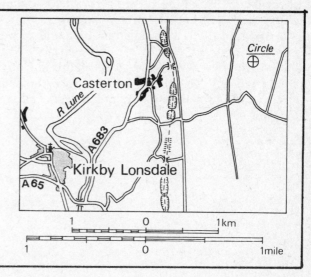

Casterton

Location: SD 639800
3.5 km (2¼ miles) NE of Kirkby
   Lonsdale
1.5 km (1 mile) E of Casterton
160 m above sea-level

In terms of the heights of its stones, the Casterton circle is the most impressive of the embanked circles. It lies 1.5 km (1 mile) east of Casterton and 2.5 km (1½ miles) south-south-east of the village of Barbon, east of the road from Kirkby Lonsdale to Sedbergh. The site is most easily reached from the trackway that passes to the east of the circle on its way up Casterton Fell. To the west of the trackway the land falls down steeply, and the stones of the circle can just be seen from the trackway standing on a level terrace on the hillside below. The land is used for rough pasture, and in places piles of stones show through the turf.

Figure 3.23 shows 19 stones forming an almost perfect circle 19 m in diameter. Although the stones are generally taller than those of the other embanked circles, they are not particularly high: the tallest stone, no. 11, measures only 50 cm, and nos. 2 and 7 just show above the level of the turf. The stones are set in an irregular bank of earth and small stones, which are most clearly visible on the western side. The bank is highest in the south and south-west where the land slopes downwards, and one of the purposes of the bank may have been to provide a level site. In the north and north-west the outer face of the bank seems to have been partially dug away; and set into the bank, just to the outside of stones 1 and 19, is a circular feature which may be the remains of a cairn. Similar features can be seen in the low bank of the Cockpit circle on Moor Divock (fig. 4.12). The inner face of the bank, just to the inside of the stone circle, is not very obvious on the ground, but it shows up well in the profile in fig. 3.23. The inner area of the circle is flat and mainly featureless, but one or two hollows may indicate the sites of opportunist digging.

No properly-conducted excavation of the circle has been recorded; but a report in the *Westmorland Advertiser and Kendal Chronicle* of 29 March 1828 tells of the finding of a number of objects at the 'Druid's Temple', situated 21 miles from Lancaster on the road to Richmond. It seem likely that the Druid's Temple is the Casterton circle.[42]

The discoveries were made by a Mr. John Tatham, and among his finds were a bronze spear-head 10 cm long, a flint arrowhead, and an 'antique drinking vessel'. The latter object may well have been a beaker.

In the late 1950s a polished jadite axehead was discovered at Moor Hall, about 1.5 km (1 mile) to the south-west of the circle.[43, 44] The axehead, presumably of neolithic date, is the first of its kind to be recorded from Cumbria. It may possibly have been connected with the circle; but if it was, the suggested early bronze age date for the circle would probably be too late. The axe can now be seen in the Craven Museum in Skipton.

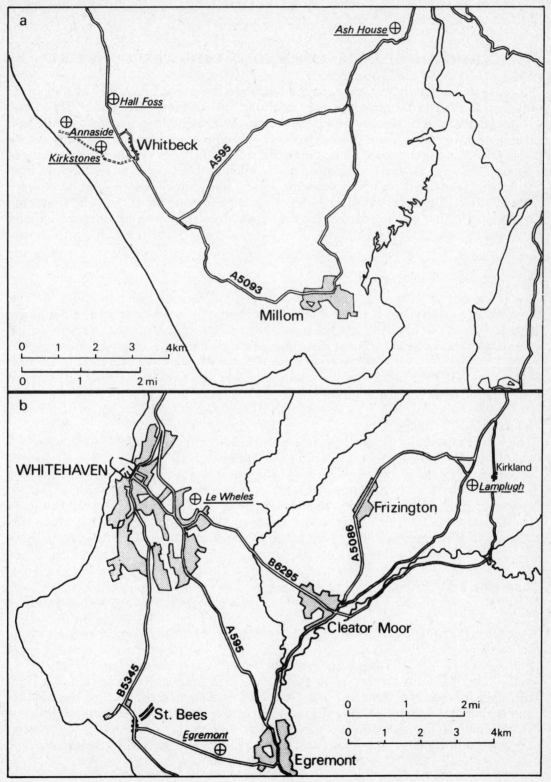

Fig. 3.24 Locations of the vanished circles of south and west Cumbria: a) SW Cumbria; b) West Cumbria.

THE VANISHED CIRCLES OF SOUTH AND WEST CUMBRIA

There is documentary evidence for the former existence of seven megalithic circles on or near the coastal plain of west Cumbria. Four of them – Annaside, Hall Foss, Kirkstones and Ash House Wood – were on the coastal strip between Bootle and Broughton (fig. 3.24a), and the three others – Lamplugh, Egremont and Le Wheles – were farther along the coast to the north (fig. 3.24b). Little or nothing now remains of them. There has always been a shortage of good arable land in west Cumbria, and any obstacle to the plough, e.g. standing stones, had slim chance of survival in times when little significance was placed on prehistoric monuments. It might be wondered how many other stone circles in Cumbria have disappeared unrecorded and unlamented.

Hall Foss SD 112857

No trace now remains of what was probably an impressive monument. It was destroyed in the late 18th or early 19th century, but we have the following description of it:[18, 45] 'At Hall Foss are the remains of a Druidical Temple called "Standing Stones" consisting of eight massive rude columns, disposed in a circle 25 yards in diameter'. The grid reference quoted above[46] places its site next to the east side of the A595 2.5 km (1½ miles) south of Bootle and 1 km (⅝ mile) north of a farm with the intriguing name of Stangrah.

Kirkstones SD 106843

The site of this circle, now utterly destroyed, is 270 m south-east of Gutterby and 1.5 km (1 mile) south-south-west of Hall Foss. It is described thus:[18, 45] 'On the Green Moor Farm are thirty stones called Kirkstones, forming part of two circles, similar in position to those of Stonehenge'. Its size is not recorded. A stylized plan shows two concentric circles,[18] making this the only such site, apart from the Druids' Circle, in south Cumbria. The circle may have been associated with a large cairn, which was apparently 200 yards (190 m) to the south of the circle and had a diameter of about 25 yards (22.5 m).[45]

Annaside SD 099853

All that is left of the circle of Annaside – a huge boulder of coursely-crystalline granite 1.37 m high and 3 m long – can be seen 1 km (⅝ mile) to the north-west of Gutterby. It stands on the edge of a gently-sloping spur overlooking a shallow valley to the north-east. The circle to which it belonged had 12 stones and a diameter of perhaps 18 m.[18, 45] The boulder bears the scars of the violence that was used to destroy its fellows – on the south-east corner is a huge hollow where it has been heavily battered. The trampled and eroded ground around the base of the boulder shows that cattle are now using it for a more prosaic purpose than that for which it was erected. In the valley on the opposite side of the spur, about 200 m to the west, are several other large granite stones, which may have belonged to the circle.

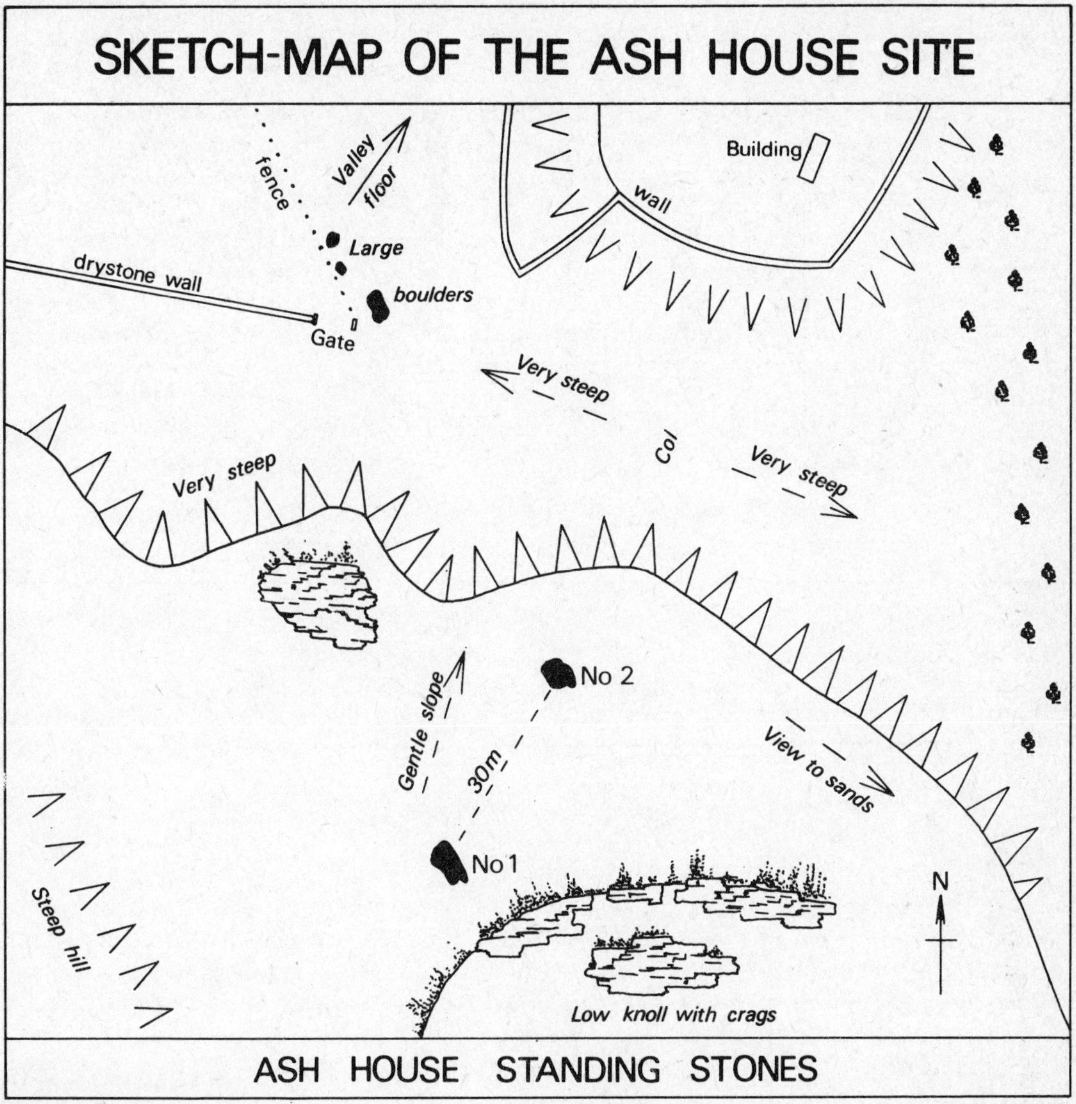

SKETCH-MAP OF THE ASH HOUSE SITE

fence

Valley floor

drystone wall

Large

boulders

Gate

Building

wall

Very steep

Col

Very steep

Very steep

No 2

Gentle slope

30m

View to sands

No 1

N

Steep hill

Low knoll with crags

ASH HOUSE STANDING STONES

No 1. looking north–west

No 2. looking north

Fig. 3.25 Site plan of the Ash House Wood stones.

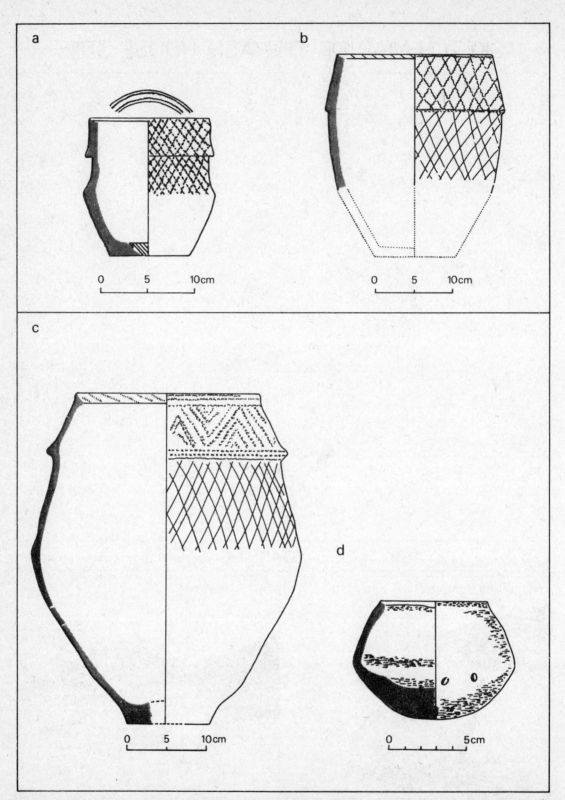

Fig. 3.26 Pottery from some Cumbria stone circles: a) Collared urn from the Druids' Circle, Birkrigg;[7] b) Collared urn from Lacra D;[17] c) Collared urn from Broomrigg C (Ch. 4, ref. 29); d) Pygmy urn from Broomrigg C (Ch. 4, ref. 29).

Ash House SD 193873

Mr. C. W. Dymond, the excavator of the Swinside circle, spent some time looking for the remains of a second megalithic circle in the parish of Millom, but apparently never succeeded. The circle has been described[47, 48] as consisting of 22 stones erected on a site seemingly levelled for the purpose. It is not surprising that Dymond was unsuccessful in his search; for only two stones now remain, and these are on the northern slopes of the Mount, near Ash House, 1 km (⅝ mile) to the east of its supposed position.

The stones are set 30 m apart on a fairly level terrace on land that slopes steeply to the south. At the bottom of the gill to the north are several other large boulders lying haphazardly (*see* fig. 3.25); they may have belonged to the circle. To the south-east the Duddon Sands are visible between the hillside and the trees. The taller stone (no. 2 on the plan) stands to a height of 1.16 m, and the other, leaning at an angle of about 45 degrees, has a height of 1.0 m. The stones appear to have been set in a layer of smaller stones, some of which are visible around the bases of the megaliths. One edge of the smaller standing stone is scarred by a set of parallel grooves about 15 cm long, which may have resulted from abortive attempts to topple the stone during the destruction of the circle.

Lamplugh NY065177

There is no description of this circle when in an undelapidated state, but from the account that does exist, it seems to have been a very impressive monument. The site of the circle is on a low hill (194 m high), 1 km (⅝ mile) north of Stockhow Hall and 4 km (2½ miles) south-west of the village of Lamplugh. Jefferson, writing of the circle in 1842,[49] states that only the northern segment then existed; the rest of the stones had been blasted and removed to make stone walls a few years previously. Six stones remained, and four of these were 'nearly 4 ft. above the ground'. They were supported by large subterranean packing stones. He estimated the diameter of the complete circle to have been '100 paces'; if so, this would make it a very large circle indeed – comparable even with Long Meg and her Daughters.

The Ringlen Stones, Egremont NX 995107

R. G. Collingwood states that this totally vanished circle was 1 mile (1.6 km) west of Egremont.[1] All that is known of it is that it consisted of 10 large stones and was '60 paces' in circumference.[50] There was apparently no evidence of an internal mound.[51]

Le Wheles NX 989180

The St Bees Register records that a building called 'Standing Stones', 1 km (⅝ mile) to the east of the centre of Whitehaven, was the site a stone circle anciently known as 'Le Wheles'. It is probably the circle referred to by R. G. Collingwood as 'Corkickle', which he states was destroyed in 1628.[1]

Chapter Four

The Stone Circles of North and East Cumbria

Introduction

The geology of the land to the east of the Cumbrian Fells in some respect mirrors that to the west. The rocks of the fells are bounded in the east by a continuation of the belt of Carboniferous limestone, wider here than in the west and north, which forms an area of elevated country rising to heights of 300 m or more. To the east of the limestone country are lower hills of Permian sandstone, which lead down to the river Eden. Separating the river from the scarp of the Pennines farther to the east is a band of Triassic sandstone. This forms a narrow strip of land at the southern end of the Eden valley, but it broadens out in the north and merges into the Carlisle lowlands. The Triassic strata are generally low-lying, but to the south-east of Carlisle they have formed into a number of hills up to 250 m high.

The river Eden has been described as 'one of the major folk-routes of prehistory'.[1] In the west the sea would have served as a major means of communication in prehistoric times. In east Cumbria this role was filled by the river Eden, which gave easy access to the lowland areas of the Eden valley. With its light, sandy soil the Eden valley provided good settlement sites, and there is also much evidence of early settlement on the limestone hills to the west of the river Eden. The Eden valley is enclosed on three sides: by the Pennines to the east, the Howgill Fells to the south, and the Cumbrian Fells to the west; so communication with other parts of the country would have been difficult. Two routes, however, were probably used. At the southern end of the Eden valley the route across Stainmore (used today by the A66) led to the Vale of York, while the Irthing valley in the north provided a way to north-east England via the Tyne Gap.

Figure 3.1 shows the locations of the stone circles in the north and east. They are concentrated in two main areas: on the limestone hills to the west of the river Eden, and on the hills of Triassic sandstone between the river Eden and the Pennines in the north. There are no known stone circles in that part of the Pennines that lie within the county of Cumbria; and there is record of only one stone circle – the destroyed site of Rawthey bridge – in the Howgill Fells. There are several categories of stone circles in the region. The open circles included the vast site of Long Meg and her Daughters and, in striking contrast, the tiny (and presumably much later) circles of Castlehowe Scar and White Hag. There are several cairn circles, two concentric circles (Gunnerkeld and Oddendale), and an embanked stone circle (Gamelands). Two henges also survive: King Arthur's Round Table and the circle-henge of Mayburgh. As in the south and west of the county, there are historical records of the destructions of a number of circles. They were destroyed for the same reasons: pressure of agriculture and their convenience as a quarry for building stone. It is likely that, as in the south and west, circles were built in this region throughout the whole of the circle-building period (fig. 2.9), and examples of some of the earliest and latest stone circles to be built lie on the hills flanking the river Eden.

The Carles, Castlerigg

Location: NY 291236
2.5 km (1½ miles) E of Keswick
215 m above sea-level

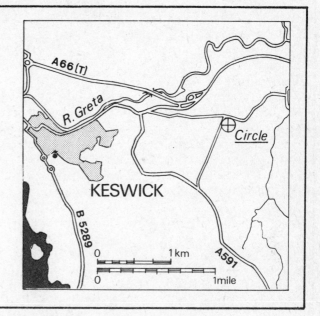

Cradled by the surrounding mountains, the great stone circle called the Carles is one of the most visually-impressive prehistoric monuments in Britain. The site is in the care of the National Trust, and it is very easily reached – a sign points the way off the A66 just to the east of Keswick. Not surprisingly, it is the most visited stone circle in Cumbria. Every year many thousands of people wander among the grey, weathered stones, taking photographs, and perhaps wondering when and by whom the circle was built.

The circle is on the level top of a low hill, Chestnut Hill, which forms part of a gentle ridge between the river Greta to the north and north-west and Naddle Beck to the east. Just to the east of the circle the land slopes down comparatively steeply. The view to the north is dominated by the three heights of Skiddaw, Blencathra and Lonscale Fell. The Derwent Fells rise to the west across Derwent Water; and Castlerigg Fell, on whose sides a fine waterfall can be seen in wet weather, encloses the site to the north.

The stones of the circle form a type A flattened ring (fig. 2.3a) with diameters 32.6 m and 29.9 m. The flattened arc is on the eastern side, where the land begins to slope downwards. Due north of the centre of the circle is an obvious entrance – a tall portal formed by stones 1 and 2, 1.72 m and 1.68 m high respectively. It is these stones that form an impressive silhouette against the sky for the visitor climbing to the circle from the minor road to the north. Another tall stone (no. 17, 1.68 m high) is almost diametrically opposite the entrance. The tallest stone, no. 14, is an irregular pillar 2.3 m high. Thirty-eight circle stones remain of an original number of forty-two or so, and all but five of them are still erect. They are set in a bed of rubble, like those

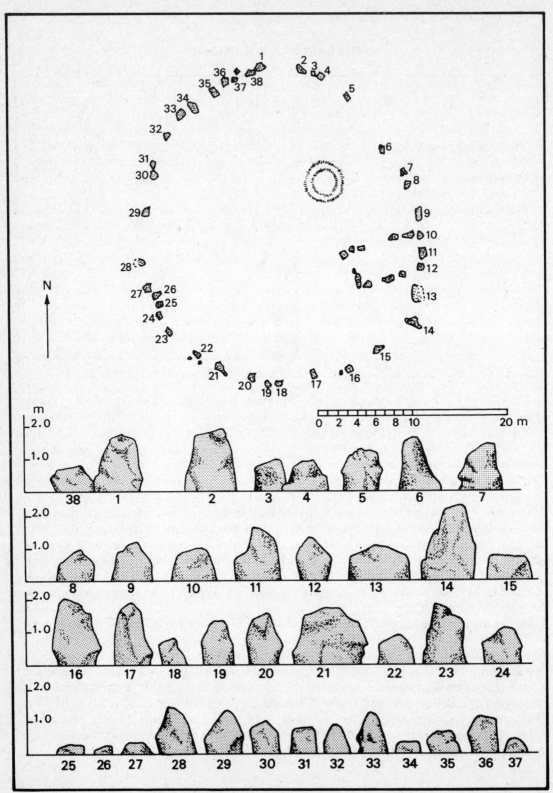

Fig. 4.1 The Carles, Castlerigg, after Dymond.[2]

of Swinside;[2] and they were probably found locally, as others have been found buried in nearby fields.[2] An enigmatic feature within the ring is a rectangle of standing stones in the south-east quadrant. There is also a faint circular feature, about 3 m across, visible in the north-east quadrant. It may be the remains of a ploughed-out barrow; for although the field is now pasture, it was under cultivation in the 17th century and the ridges and furrows left by the plough are still visible near the circle. It is by no means certain, however, that the circular feature was a burial mound.

Like so many other open stone circles, little has been found here to indicate its age and purpose. Its architecture points to an early date, and Burl suggests it is one of the earliest stone circles in Britain.[3] It may have been built around the beginning of the later neolithic period, around 3000BC. Williams reported in 1856 that three cairns existed within the circle,[4] but there is now no trace of them. Whether they had a sepulchral use is not known; they may simply have been piles of stones removed from the field, as was probably the case with the 'cairns' within Long Meg and her Daughters. The only artifacts recorded from within the circle are three Cumbrian stone axes. Two of these were mentioned by Williams;[4] he described one as a 'rude stone club' (probably a roughed-out stone axe) and the other as a stone celt (a polished stone axe). The third was an unpolished stone axe, 21 cm long, found in 1875.[5] The presence of these axes is quite consistent with an early date for the circle.

In 1882 Mr. Kinsey Dover excavated within the rectangle of stones in order to find evidence for its use; but to this end he was unsuccessful. All he discovered was a pit, about 1 m deep, filled with earth, stones, and pieces of charcoal. There is nothing quite like the rectangle in any other stone circle in the British Isles. The closest parallels are provided by the two rectangular settings of stone slabs found buried within the circles of Stenness in the Orkneys[6a] and Balbirnie in Fife.[6b] It seems possible that these are related to the rectangular timber mortuary enclosures that have been found under several neolithic long and round barrows.

It is not surprising that such a well-known and impressive stone circle has attracted the attentions of investigators looking for astronomical significance in megalithic sites. Alexander Thom has studied the site in detail, and he considers it to be a most important one in terms of megalithic astronomy and geometry; for the basic geometric construction seems to have built into it significant astronomical alignments. He is impressed by the remarkable way in which 'the geometry of a Type A construction has been made to serve astronomical requirements'.[7] One of the two main axes of the geometrical construction of the Type A circle (fig. 2.3a) passes through stones 32 and 14 (the tallest stone) and the main centre of the circle. This aligns to the south-east with the rising of the sun over High Rigg on Candlemas – one of the quarter days of Thom's 16-month megalithic calendar.[8] Extended in the opposite direction, the alignment marks the position of the sun setting over the western flank of Skiddaw at the summer solstice. The position of the mid-winter rising sun is indicated by an alignment from the centre of the circle to stone 15. Thom also gives significant lunar alignments from the centre of the circle to perimeter stones.[8]

On the western edge of the field, by a stile, is a stone standing to a height of about 1 m. It is 90 m west-south-west of the centre of the circle. Thom considered this to be an outlier of the circle, and that an alignment between it, the centre of the circle, and stone 8 had calendrical significance.[9] The stone, however, is not in its original position, so its astronomical significance is doubtful. It is scarred by parallel scratches caused by ploughing (see plate 11), which show that it was at one time buried;[10] and it is reported to have once been farther from the circle than it is at present.[11]

Suggestions, by Anderson, of a much more speculative and imaginative nature, have been made for the astronomical use for the site. He believed that one of the main purposes of the circle was for the construction of a 'Celtic Kalendar' in order to fix feast-days.[11] He pointed out that the notch in the top of stone 23 could be conveniently used for sighting across the ring to stone 6, which is suitably pointed. Extension of this line to the horizon gave the rising position of the sun at the summer solstice. His most interesting alignment was between a second outlier and the centre of the circle. This outlier is no longer visible. It lay 61 m west-south-west of the centre, and in 1914 it was almost buried with its top broken off.[11] The alignment extended all the way to distant Fiend's Fell in the Pennines, and it indicated the rising point of the sun on or around May Day. Perhaps by strange coincidence, the line passes through the centre of Long Meg and her Daughters; for it coincides exactly with Thom's alignment from the Long Meg circle via Little Meg to Fiend's Fell (p. 104).

It seems that at one time there was another stone circle nearby. William Stukeley, writing in the first half of the 18th century, mentions a second 'Druidical circle' in the next field towards Keswick,[12] but a century later there was no sign of it.[4]

Long Meg and her Daughters

Location: NY 571372
10 km (6¼ miles) NE of Penrith
175 m above sea-level

Little Meg

Location: NY577375
170 m above sea-level

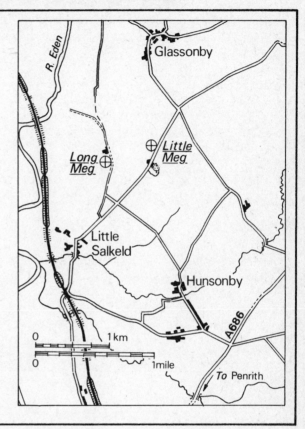

Long Meg and her Daughters

Long Meg and her Daughters (see plate 12) is one of the largest stone circles in Britain: only Stanton Drew in Somerset and the outer stone circle at Avebury are larger. Long Meg is a menhir, a column of Triassic sandstone 3.7 m high, standing a short distance to the south-west of the circle. Her daughters, the stones of the circle, are reputedly a coven of witches turned to stone by a magician as they celebrated their sabbat.

The circle lies 1 km (⅝ mile) to the east of the river Eden, on a low, broad plateau of elevated land, on which are also the nearby circles of Little Meg and Glassonby. The site is easily visited. A sign points the way off the Glassonby to Little Salkeld road along a side-road, which passes through the eastern half of the circle on its way to Longmeg Farm just beyond; it is therefore possible to drive right into the ring. The side-road climbs up from the road below, and the first evidence of the circle is the sight of Long Meg herself rising above the level of an intervening stone wall. The stones of the circle are not visible until the top of the hill is reached. This may give a clue to the significance of Long Meg. To someone climbing up to the circle from the river Eden, which in prehistoric times would have provided a convenient means of

99

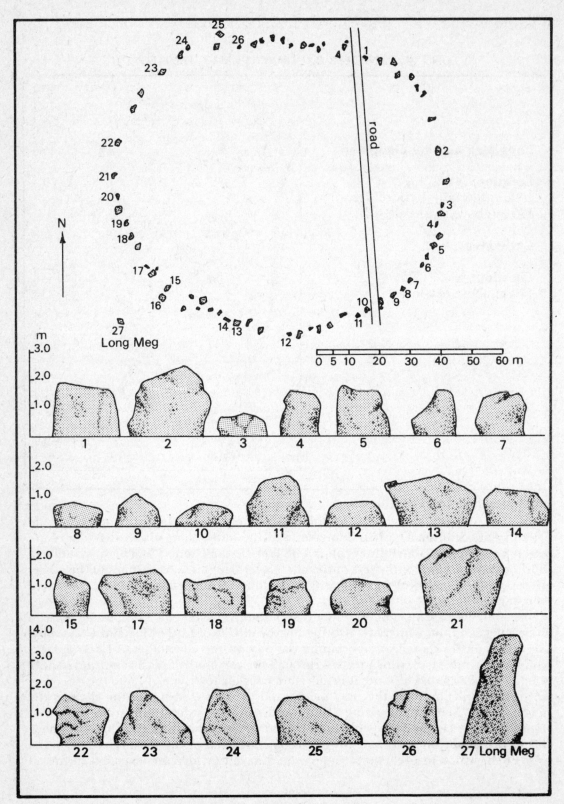

Fig. 4.2 Long Meg and her Daughters, after Dymond.[2]

travel, the circle would have been hidden behind the crest of the hill. Long Meg, however, is tall enough to have been visible from below, and it would have shown the way.

The site of the circle is not level: the land slopes downwards to the north and north-east. The stones of the south-west arc are on higher land than the rest, and they form the local skyline for someone standing in the centre of the circle. This huge ring is made of 69 stones, and originally there were probably more. But be careful should you decide to count the stones! Tradition claims that if you count the same total twice, the enchantment that holds the witches in their petrified stance will be broken. Although one feels dwarfed by the size of the stones, when one looks across the circle from one side to the other the stones are themselves dwarfed by the scale of the structure that they form. Yet for all its grandeur, the circle lacks the charming intimacy of the Carles or Swinside. The ring has a flattened arc in the north, and Thom[13] classes it as a Type B flattened circle (fig. 2.3a). Its diameters are 109 m from east to west and 93 m from north to south. The size of the ring is reflected in the immensity of the stones. Twenty-seven stones are still standing, and of these several are over 2 m tall. The largest of the standing stones is no. 13; it is 3.3 m wide and estimated to weigh 28 tons. It would have required 120 people to set it up.[14] Two other large stones, nos. 2 and 18, mark the two ends of Thom's primary diameter in his Type B construction.[9] The presence of the two stones at these positions lends support for Thom's geometrical interpretation.

The circle has several interesting features. In the south-west is an entrance consisting of two pairs of stones, almost identical to that at Swinside. The presence of Long Meg to the outside of the entrance supports the idea that the menhir was used as a direction indicator. The stones of the western arc can be seen to be set in a low bank about 3.5 m wide but now only a few centimetres high. It is not known whether the bank ever extended around the whole of the circle, or indeed if it was ever much higher than it is now. The bank is not as evident as that of the embanked stone circle of Gamelands, but it may possibly indicate a connection between Long Meg and her Daughters and the henge-building tradition.

The flattened arc in the north is formed from irregularly-set stones. It starts from around stone 24, at a point where two arcs seem to overlap. If the arc indicated by stones 24 and 25 is continued round to the east of stone 1, it would be well outside Thom's geometrical construction. The present arrangement may be the result of a change of plan on the part of the builders; or it might have been caused by more modern interference. A folktale relates how several stones were shifted to improve the yield of the crop. This had a deleterious effect, however, as no crop at all was obtained; so the stones were replaced.[15] A historical record of destruction is provided by William Stukeley, who visited the site in 1725.[16] He reported that several of the stones had been recently removed by blasting, and others had been cut up and used as millstones.

No excavations have been carried out here, nor is there any verifiable report of finds from the circle. The inner area is devoid of any trace of burial mound or any other feature. Camden, in his 'Britannia' of 1599, mentions two heaps of stones within the circle; but an editorial note in a later edition of the book states that the mounds had nothing to do with the circle, and that they were merely stones gathered from the surrounding field.[17] John Aubrey makes an uncertain reference to the find of 'giants' bones' within the circle in his 'Monumenta Britannica' of 1650.

Long Meg herself is worth a close inspection. It is 72.6 m from the centre of the circle, from where the sun will be seen to set behind the menhir on the winter solstice. On its weathered north-eastern side, the side facing the entrance, are three sets of incised carvings. Although they are now very faint, their shapes can still be discerned. The lowest of the three consists of four concentric circles, the outer being 25 cm in diameter (see plate 13). Superimposed on the bottom of the outer circle are segments of two other concentric circles of an incomplete lower group. Above this set are three concentric circles 19 cm across carved around a central depression (cup-mark). To the right of this composition, and slightly lower down the stone, is a barely-recognisable spiral.

Stukeley makes reference to a stone circle in the adjoining field to the south-west.[18] It consisted of 20 stones and was about 15 m in diameter. It also had an outlier, and it seems to have been a miniature version of its much larger neighbour. No trace of it now remains. A drawing, made by Stukeley in 1725, of Long Meg and her Daughters shows the smaller circle in the backgound, at a point where there is now a farm building.[19] Just beyond this circle, the land begins to slope down to the river Eden.

Let us leave the last words to William Wordsworth, who first visited Long Meg and her Daughters in 1833. In a note appended to the poem from which the lines below are taken, he tells us that he came upon the monument by surprise. The sight made a deep impression on him. He says of it 'I have not seen any other relique of those dark ages which can pretend to rival it in singularity and dignity of appearance'. The opening lines of the poem inspired by the encounter, however, reveal a more sinister emotion.

> 'A weight of awe, not easy to be borne,
> Fell suddenly upon my spirit – cast
> From the dread bosom of the unknown past,
> When first I saw that family forlorn.'

Little Meg

Just over 0.5 km (⅓ mile) to the north-east of Long Meg and her Daughters, the largest stone circle in Cumbria, is one of the smallest. It is appropriately named Little Meg, but is referred to by some authors, less descriptively, as the Maughanby circle. Obscured by long grass and nettles, the circle is 150 m to the west of the road from Little Salkeld to Glassonby, near the edge of a pasture field. There is a convenient access to the circle through a gate by the roadside.

Little Meg is now unfortunately a confusion of stones, owing to its being in a convenient spot to deposit troublesome stones from the field. The largest stone at the centre of the circle certainly does not belong there, as it is criss-crossed by plough marks. Dymond's plan of 1875,[20] reproduced in fig. 4.3, shows 11 stones forming an irregular ring measuring 5.86 m by 4.72 m around a cist, which was covered by a mound of earth. There is now no trace of the mound, but some of the stones in the

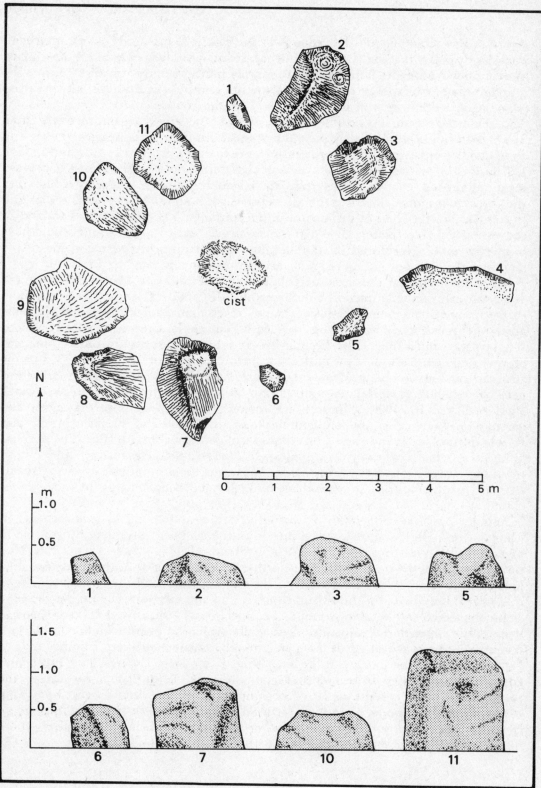

Fig. 4.3 Little Meg, after Dymond.[20]

centre of the circle may be the remains of the cist. It is reported that an interment was found within the cist,[21] but no further details are given. There are now many more stones within the boundary of the circle than are shown in fig. 4.3, but the original stones can still be discerned, sometimes with difficulty. Partially covering stone no. 4 is the largest of the newcomers, a large granite boulder.

Considering the small size of the circle, many of the stones are impressively large. The tallest is no. 11, a great rectangular stone 1.3 m high and measuring over 1 m across its flat top. Many of the prostrate stones are also very large; no. 9 is 2 m long, and no. 2 is 1.8 m, and they may have risen higher than no. 11 when erect. No. 2 is the most interesting of the stones. On its bevelled shoulder, plainly visible, is a well-executed geometrical carving. It consists of a spiral linked to a set of five concentric circles. The outer diameter of the spiral and the circles are 13 cm and 22 cm respectively (see plate 14). When the stone was vertical, the carving would have been very strikingly placed on the sloping upper surface. Apparently one of the stones of the cist, now removed, was carved with cup-and-ring marks.[22]

Is it significant that the three neighbouring circles of Long Meg, Little Meg and Glassonby are the only ones in Cumbria known to sport carvings? Does it imply a connection between them in terms of culture or ceremony? Little Meg and Glassonby are both probably of early bronze age date, and could have been constructed at roughly the same time. But Long Meg and her Daughters is older, and was constructed centuries, if not a millenium, before its smaller neighbours. It may be that the carvings on Long Meg herself were made long after the great circle was constructed; but as spiral markings occur at the neolithic site of New Grange (radiocarbon date 2400bc), there is no obvious reason to suppose that circle and carvings at Long Meg are not contemporary. Cup-and-ring marks, spirals, and related designs are found carved on stones throughout the British Isles. The purpose of these enigmatic carvings is unknown, although several plausible (and not so plausible) suggestions have been made. Whatever their significance was, it seems that for many centuries they held meaning for the people living in this part of Cumbria.

Another possible connection between Little Meg and Long Meg is revealed in Thom's work. He has shown that a line from the centre of the Long Meg circle to Fiend's Fell passes through Little Meg.[23] (Fiend's Fell is visible from Little Meg through a gap in the trees to the east-north-east, over the gate at the roadside.) The alignment indicated the rising point of the sun on or around the two quarter days that fall midway between the spring equinox and summer solstice and between the summer solstice and autumn equinox. These are two of the days that Thom used to define his 16-month 'megalithic' calendar, for which he gives evidence in his first book.[24] The presence of Little Meg on this alignment may seem coincidental, as Little Meg would be too low to be seen from Long Meg. However, the alignment could have been used from Little Meg in the opposite direction, to observe the setting point of the sun on the two other quarter days. The line of sight from Little Meg to Long Meg is now blocked by trees. Whether the line of sight was open when the circle was in use, and if so, whether the alignment was used for this purpose, are questions that are probably impossible to answer.

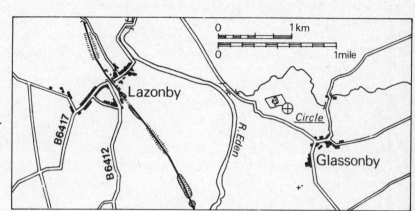

Glassonby

Location: NY 573393
2.5 km (1½ miles) SE of
 Kirkoswald
130 m above sea-level

The site of this circle is a short distance to the north-west of the village of Glassonby, and is just over 2 km (1¼ miles) to the north of Long Meg and her Daughters. Access to the circle is through a gate on the side of the road from Glassonby to Kirkoswald, near the village boundary of Glassonby. From a distance the stone circle seems to form a kerb of contiguous stones around the base of a low mound, but on closer inspection the mound is seen to extend beyond the stones. In fact, until its excavation by W. G. Collingwood in 1900,[25] the stones of the circle were covered by the mound, and they were only revealed on removal of the water-worn cobbles from which the mound was constructed. Other stone circles are known to exist under burial mounds, such as that under a tumulus on Birkrigg Common (p. 38).

The mound and circle are set on the flat top of a slight rise. The land slopes gently down on three sides and down more steeply to the north to a small plantation a few metres away. Melmerby Fell in the Pennines dominates the scene to the east; and to the west, across the Eden valley, are the most northerly of the Lakeland Fells.

The stones of the circle are of several types, including sandstones, grits and granite. They form an oval, possibly even an egg-shape, measuring 15.7 m by 14 m. The tallest stone is no. 6 (92 cm). The inner flat face of stone 28 has a number of faint, lichen-shrouded markings. When the stone was first revealed, the design was seen to consist of four concentric circles 21 cm across, with two groups of concentric semicircles above,[22] producing a 'Mickey Mouse'-like appearance. The present state of the circle (fig. 4.4) is virtually as shown on Collingwood's plan, except that stone 21 has been pushed down the mound, and no. 20 has been slightly displaced.

On excavating the mound, Collingwood found a burial cist within the circle, 6 m south-west of the centre.[25] The remains of the cist are still visible on the inside of the gap between stones 1 and 30. The cist was empty, but two cremations were

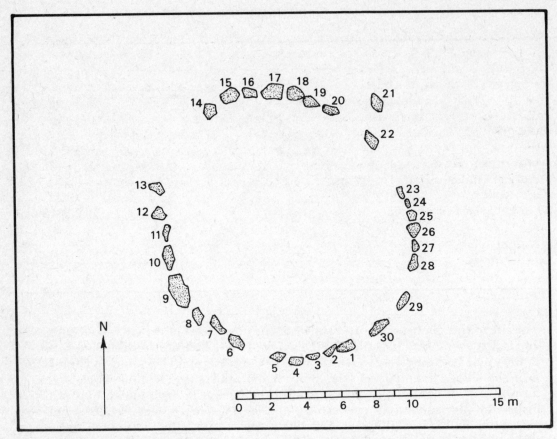

Fig. 4.4   Glassonby, after Collingwood.

discovered under the mound just outside the circle. One was by stone 20, and the other, contained in a collared urn, was outside the gap between stones 28 and 29. A bead of light blue faience was also discovered. The bead and urn, now in Carlisle Museum, indicate an early bronze age date for the site.

The Broomrigg circles are in a similar situation to that of Grey Yauds, 2 km (1¼ miles) to the north (p. 151). They are on a low hill of Triassic sandstone between the Pennines to the east and the river Eden to the west. There are the remains of four stone circles of various types here (sites A, B, C and D); and excavations carried out in the vicinity have found further evidence of prehistoric activity. Among the sites discovered are a bronze age habitation (site F),[26] which may have been connected with the circles, and a beaker burial (site N).[27] The excavations were carried out when the land was open; however, the whole area is now covered by a young conifer plantation, and in consequence access is severely limited. Circles A and B can still be visited without undue trouble, but the other two circles are now lost among the trees.

Broomrigg A NY 548467 (see plate 15)
The remains of this ring can be reached by walking along the western side of the stone wall that leads southwards from the road alongside the plantation. Its stones can be glimpsed disappearing into the trees to the right of the wall 660 m from the road.

It must have been by far the largest of the four circles; and as there is no indication that it contained a burial, it is probably the earliest, although there is no direct evidence to confirm this. The plan of the circle drawn in 1934[28] shows the stones arranged in a much-elongated circle having a maximum diameter from north-east to south-west of about 50 m (fig. 4.6). A possible avenue of stones 35 m wide was also found, leading away to the north-west. The larger stones of the northern arc still survive, probably in their original positions, but only three of them stand over 50 cm high. The stones of the avenue can also be traced; but the southern arc of the circle has been much disturbed. Although several stones in this part of the ring are still visible, they are loose and their positions no longer accord with those in fig. 4.6.

A limited excavation was carried out in 1950,[26] before the planting of the trees. At this time the land was open heath. The stones of the circle were found to be set 20-25 cm into the ground in prepared socket-holes packed with small stones. No artefacts or other datable material were found.

It is difficult to be sure of the original appearance of the circle – it may have been an ellipse – but it was certainly very large. The excavator thought that it would have been similar to the destroyed circle of Grey Yauds.

Broomrigg B NY548466
This is the smallest of the four Broomrigg circles. It lies 100 m to the south of Broomrigg A, and like the latter it is visible from the edge of the woods by the western side of the stone wall. It is a cairn circle, but only four of the original seven stones remain; they form a small circle of diameter 3.4 m. Stones 2, 3 and 4, all hard red sandstone, are erect; but no. 1, a light-coloured sandstone, has fallen. Traces of

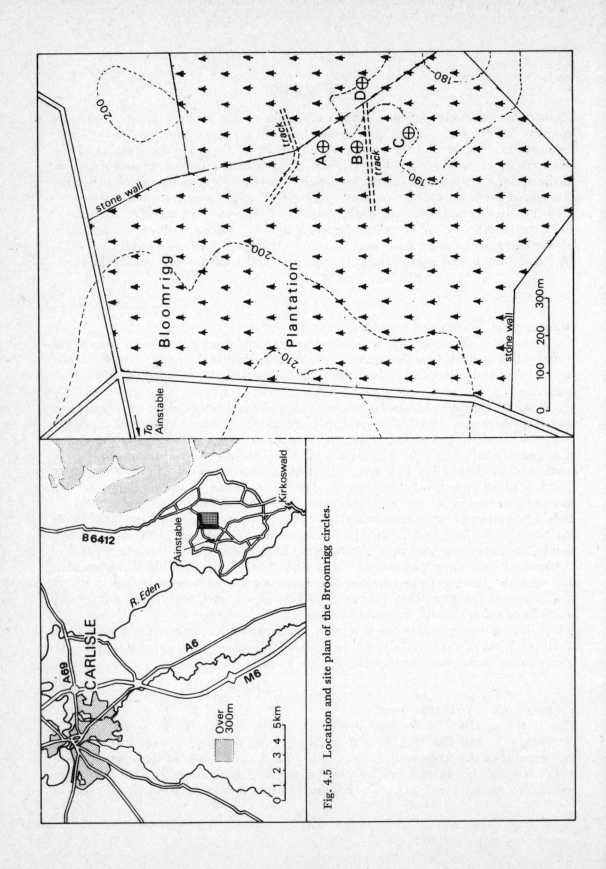

Fig. 4.5 Location and site plan of the Broomrigg circles.

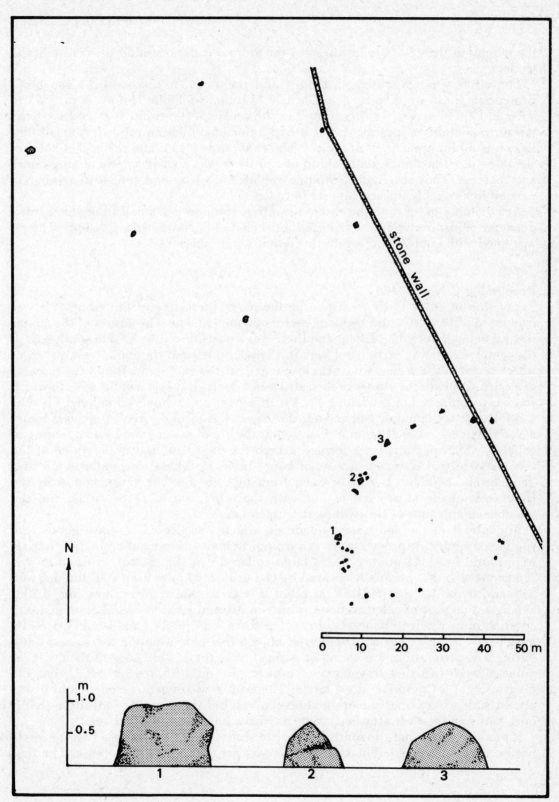

Fig. 4.6 Broomrigg A, after Hodgson.[28]

the mound of the cairn are visible, and the ground is depressed in the centre of the circle.

The circle was excavated in 1950,[26] and the finds, like those from the other Broomrigg sites, are displayed in Carlisle Museum in Tullie House. A pit 0.53 m deep and 1.6 m across was discovered in the centre of the circle. It must have been meant to contain an interment, but it had unfortunately been robbed. A small flint flake was all that remained in the pit. The excavators also found the socket holes of the three missing stones, and behind one of these was a small pit containing bones and charcoal. They also found a strange, rounded block of sandstone with a design of crossed lines deeply incised into its flat face.

At a distance of 7.6 m to the east, a tiny circle composed of small stones and with a diameter of just over 1 m was reported. Like circle B it contained a small pit. The pit was lined with cobbles, but again its contents were missing.

Broomrigg C NY 548465

Excavation of circle C showed it to be the most interesting of the group.[29] It was composed of 14 stones and had a diameter of about 15.6 m. The largest of the stones was 1.2 m long, but it had fallen; and there was a possible outlier 14.5 m south-east of the centre. Work was carried out here in 1948-9. Starting at the south-west quadrant where seven of the stones were set close together, the excavators found the remains of a cairn. Beneath the stones of the cairn was a deep pit (point *a* in fig. 4.8), in which was a cist composed of sandstone slabs with a great cover-stone 1.5 m long. The cist was found to contain only soil and a little charcoal. A second, wrecked cist was found a short distance away at point *h*. Just within the arc of seven stones was a footing of cobbles, which perhaps once formed a kerb for the cairn; and under three of the cobbles were two compact masses of bone (point *b*). These were interpreted as a 'foundation sacrifice'. It can be seen from fig. 4.8 that the seven stones of the south-west quadrant are out of line with the other stones of the circle, and the possible significance of this will be discussed later.

In contrast to the south-west quadrant, which was devoid of grave goods, the south-east quadrant proved more rewarding. Remains of several cremation burials were found here. At point *c* was a large collared urn (fig. 3.26c), crushed by the sandstone slab that originally covered it. The urn would have been 40.6 cm high and 25.4 cm across its rim. Nearby, at point *d*, was an intact pygmy urn (fig. 3.26d) amongst a deposit of calcined bone. Thirteen discs of jet were found among stones covering more calcined bone at point *e*. The discs were pierced and would originally have been strung as beads. Another jet object, this time a button 3 cm across and having a V-perforation, was found at point *f*. Near the eastern edge of the circle, at point *g*, were two tiny fragments of bronze, the only bronze recorded from the excavation of a Cumbrian stone circle. The bronze was much corroded, and it was not possible to say what the original object was; but there was an indication that it once had some leather attached, so it may have been a knife or an awl.

It was suggested that the south-west arc of stones provides evidence that the circle has been reconstructed. The course of events may have been as follows. The first

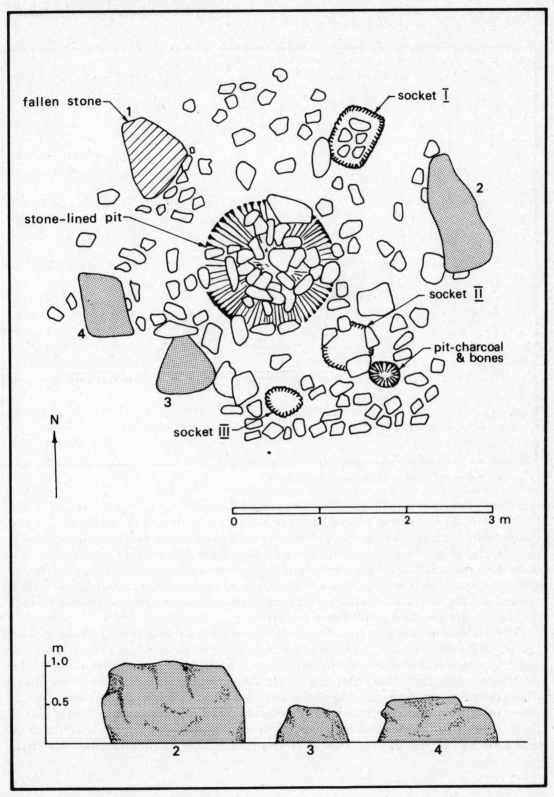

fallen stone

socket $\overline{\text{I}}$

1

2

stone-lined pit

socket $\overline{\text{II}}$

4

pit-charcoal
& bones

3

socket $\overline{\text{III}}$

N

0   1   2   3 m

m

1.0

0.5

2

3

4

Fig. 4.7 Broomrigg B, after Hodgson.[26]

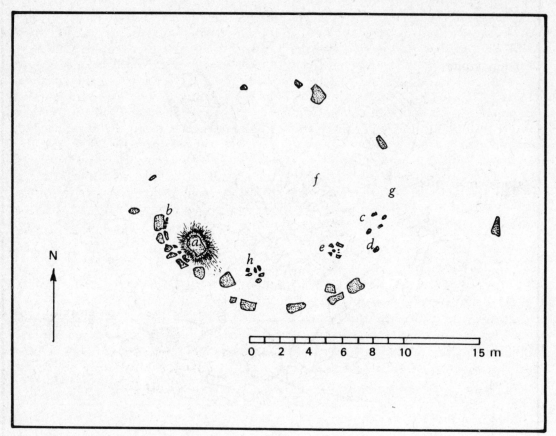

Fig. 4.8 Broomrigg C, after Hodgson and Harper.[29]

stage was the erection of a small stone circle of diameter 4.3 m. A pit was dug in the centre, and an interment placed in a cist within; a cairn was then raised over the grave. This cairn circle would have been of similar size to the neighbouring circles B and D, and also to the cairn circle of Little Meg 9 km (5½ miles) to the south. At a later date the small circle was demolished, apart from the south-west arc, which was incorporated into a newly-constructed larger circle. More interments were then placed within the new sanctuary. This suggested reconstruction is similar to that postulated for the Brat's Hill circle (p. 56).

The finds from circle C are all datable to the early bronze age, i.e. from around 2400 to 1600BC; but is it possible to be more precise about when the circle was in use? V-perforated buttons of the type found here were formerly thought to be indicative of Beaker associations; and the Beaker culture was considered to have flourished right at the beginning of the early bronze age. Beaker burials usually, but not exclusively, contain crouched inhumations and not cremations with collared urns, a practice that became increasingly popular later in the early bronze age. The juxtaposition of the button, calcined bone and collared urn would on this basis indicate use of the circle over several centuries during the early bronze age, even after any reconstruction took place.[29] Such an interpretation, however, may be no longer valid. Radiocarbon dating indicates that beaker burials took place throughout most of the early bronze age from roughly 2100-1450bc; and V-perforated buttons seem to occur mainly in the middle to later stages of the early bronze age, from 1800bc onwards.[30] Also, V-perforated buttons have been found in non-beaker contexts in conjunction with cremation in collared urns in barrows belonging to the Wessex culture in southern England. In the light of this evidence, it seems that Broomrigg C was more likely to have been in use over a much shorter period of time than the original argument suggested; and the various finds do not necessarily indicate use of the circle by successive cultures. A date in the second half of the early bronze age, say around 1600bc (c.1950BC), seems more probable. In line with this, a radiocarbon date of 1670bc has been obtained from the Amesbury 39 barrow in Wiltshire,[31] which contained jet beads and a V-perforated button.

Broomrigg D NY 550466
This small circle was the last of the group to be excavated (1960).[27] It was an irregular circle measuring 5.5 m from north to south and 4.5 m from east to west. All the stones were prostrate; the largest was 1.6 m long, but it may never have been erect, as no socket hole was found for it. No bones or cinerary urns were found here; and the only discoveries were a few shards of pottery and some worked flakes of flint, one of which was a blade 6 cm long.

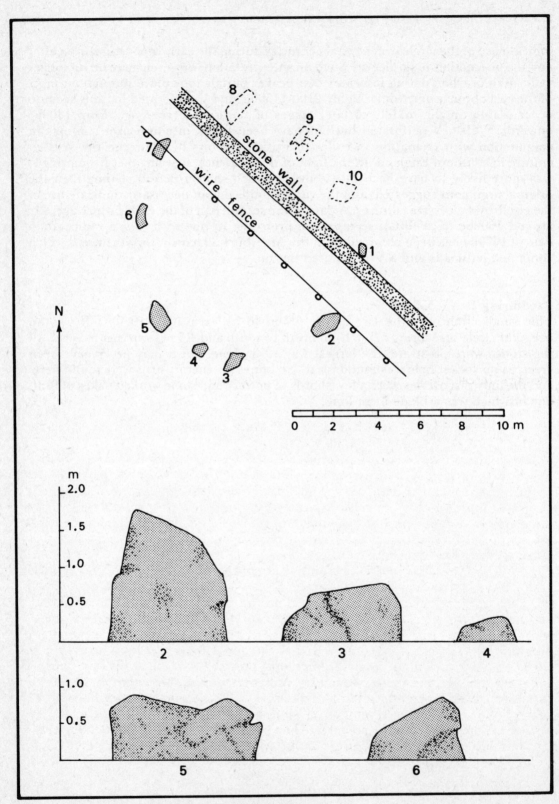

Fig. 4.9 Leacet Hill, after Robinson and Ferguson.[32]

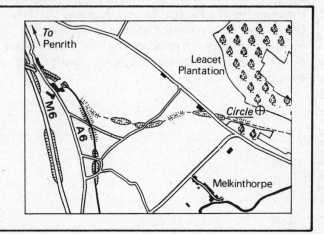

Leacet Hill

Location: NY 563263
On edge of Leacet Plantation
6.5 km (4 miles) SE of Penrith
135 m above sea-level

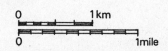

This cairn circle is sited at the base of Leacet Hill, from which it gets its name, on the southern boundary of Leacet Hill plantation. The stones of the cairn can be seen from the Cilburn to Penrith road at the point where the road crosses the embankment of a dismantled railway. The most convenient approach to the site is by the new forest track, which starts just opposite the junction with the road to Melkinthorpe and Lowther. The track passes through the woods by the road, over the railway embankment, and then through a new conifer plantation and up the slope to the old plantation of Leacet Hill. The circle is 225 m to the east of the track, along the drystone boundary wall of the plantation.

The drystone wall and accompanying wire fence pass through the circle. There is now little to be seen of the circle on the plantation side of the wall; but in front of the wall five large stones remain, set in a semicircle round the top of the cairn, which is hollowed in the centre. The cairn forms a small, level platform on the hillside, and has a sharply-sloping edge to the outside of stones 3 to 5. The land slopes down to the south-west across pasture to the new plantation, and rises immediately to the north and east up Leacet Hill.

The plan of the circle in fig. 4.9 is adapted from that drawn by J. B. Harvey in 1880 at the time of the excavation of the circle.[32] Stones 8, 9 and 10 were found buried, and no. 9 had been split by tree roots. Stone no. 1 can still be located just behind the wall, and no. 7 is obscured by grass beneath the wire fence. The tallest stone is no. 2, which is 1.25 m high. The original diameter of the circle would have been about 11.5 m; however, the shape is not a true circle, and Thom classifies it as a Type II egg.[33] This is a rare shape, and Thom records only three others in his first book.

Excavation of the site by Robinson and Ferguson showed that it had been extensively used for cremated burial. Pottery vessels containing cremated bones had been placed at the feet of several of the stones, a feature reminiscent of Lacra D. In all, five collared urns (one by stones 6, 8 and 9 and two by stone 2), a food vessel and a pygmy cup (both by stone 8), were found. All the vessels contained calcined bone.

115

One of the urns by stone 2 had been inverted over its contents, and the rest were upright. In the centre of the circle the excavators found what they considered to be the remains of a funeral pyre: a layer of charcoal, possibly beech, containing calcined bones and fire-reddened stones. Whether the stones of the circle had but one brief moment of glory – a great cremation, bones placed into vessels and carefully buried – or whether the interments were made over a period of time, is a matter for speculation.

Moor Divock is a featureless tract of fairly level, elevated land, 300 m above sea-level, forming part of Askham Fell. In 19th-century texts the name is sometimes rendered Muir Divock or Moor Doveack. Turf and bracken cover the peaty moor, which in places is very boggy. To the east the land slopes down to Askham and Helton, and beyond to the river Lowther. To the west and south-west the elevation of the land rises to the notable peaks of Loadpot Hill and Arthur's Pike, before falling rapidly down to Ullswater. In the distance to the north-west, just visible over the local skyline, are the twin peaks of Blencathra. Access to the moor is easiest from the delightful village of Helton, about 9 km (5½ miles) to the north-west of Shap. A well-defined trackway over the moor passes close to most of the sites described here.

The acid, peaty soils of the moor are not suitable for agriculture, and the main use for the land is now sheep-grazing and grouse shooting. There is, however, plentiful evidence of prehistoric occupation here. Dotted about the moor are many cairns and burial mounds; the most conspicuous of these is White Raise, which is near the junction of the trackway over the moor and the path to Askham. Within this mound a cist was found containing human bones.[34,41] Just to the east of the trackway are the remains of two small stone circles (Moor Divock 4 and 5), and to the west of the trackway is a settlement site consisting of hut-circles and tumuli.[35] The Cockpit, by far the largest and most impressive of the Moor Divock circles, is about 1 km to the west of the two smaller circles. It is likely that the stone circles and burial mounds belong to the early bronze age, and it is possible that the settlement may be connected with them.

What now remains of the bronze age structures is but a small fraction of what was visible in the second half of the 19th century, if Taylor's detailed account was accurate.[34] Strung out over the moor, between the Kopstone and White Raise (a distance of just over 1 km (¾ mile), were nine small stone circles (some concentric rings) and cairn-circles. Linking several of the circles was a 'serpentine' avenue of low stones, running parallel with the trackway for a distance of about 500 m. There is now no definite trace of this avenue, and its former existence has been questioned.[36] Of the nine circles mentioned by Taylor, only one of them (no. 4) is recognisable, and there are the remains of a possible second (no. 5).

It is impossible to know what credence to give to Taylor's account; even his plan[34] of circle 4 bears only slight resemblance to the actual object. It is fairly certain, however, that the cairns and stone circles have been subject to much disturbance over the last century. When Taylor wrote his account in 1886, he noted that circle 5 had been delapidated 25 years previously. It is possible that the stones from several of Taylor's circles and the avenue were used in the construction of hides for grouse shooters. Some of the present hides look surprisingly like the hollow-centred burial cairns in the area. Even circle 4 may have been remodelled for use as a hide; and if this were so, it might account for the difference between its present appearance and Taylor's plan of it.

The Kopstone is a gnarled standing stone, 1.65 m high, atop a low hill, and it is clearly visible from a long distance in all directions. There are several versions of its

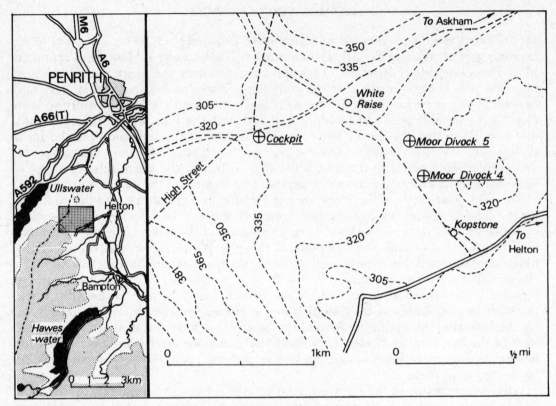

Fig. 4.10   Location and site plan of the Moor Divock circles.

name: Cop Stone, Copt Stone and Cockstone. Since its erection it has probably been an important direction indicator and a place for meeting. Sports were apparently held by the stone up to 1880,[37] and local tradition also claims that the Shap avenue actually extended to it.[38] Taylor described the Kopstone as being the largest remaining member of a stone circle of diameter 17.4 m, built around a ring-mound. There is now litle evidence of the supposed structure, apart perhaps from a slight circular bank that is visible in places.

Moor Divock 4 NY494220
This circle is designated as Moor Divock f by the Royal Commission for Ancient and Historic Monuments.[36] It is 440 m north-west of the Kopstone, from which it is clearly visible. Midway between the two is a group of large boulders (one of which is split), which may have been artificially raised. Moor Divock 4 is a cairn circle (fig. 2.1d) and is marked as such on the Ordnance Survey maps. It consists of a ring of 10 large stones set in a bank of smaller stones around the top of a cairn, which measures about 11.5 m across its base. The 10 stones vary in height from 32 cm (no. 5) to 97 cm (no. 8), and only two of them are still standing vertically (nos. 1 and 8). There is a

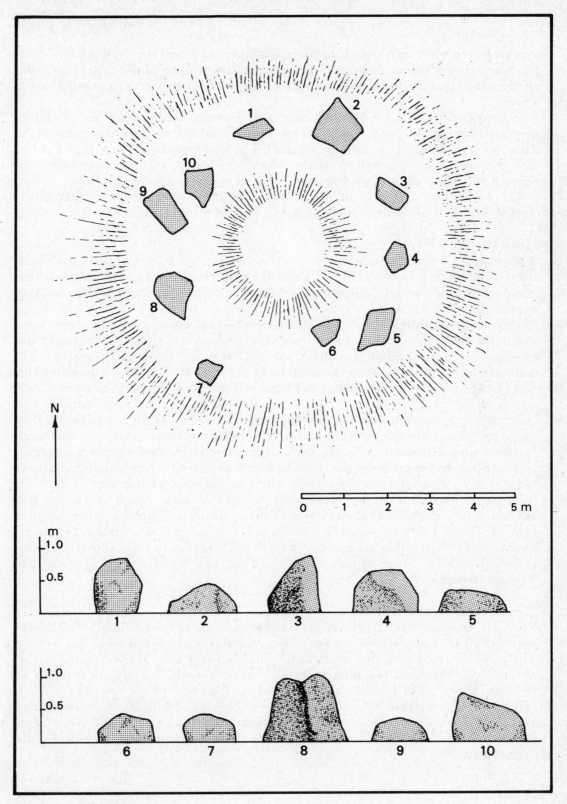

Fig. 4.11 Moor Divock 4.

pronounced projection of rubble between stones 6 and 7, and the circular area within the stone ring is deeply hollowed. The present appearance of the cairn circle may partly result from its excavation and also, as suggested above, from its possible use as a hide.

Canons Greenwell and Simpson[39] excavated the cairn in May 1866, and it 'yielded up the story of its purpose'.[34] A food vessel was found 60 cm below the centre of the cairn, lying on its side in a layer of fine sand. The food vessel was 14 cm high and had four unpierced lugs attached to its shoulders.[40] Beneath the layer of sand were the burnt bones of an adult. Two fragments of a second vessel were also found.

The stones now surround an empty tomb. Do they appeal to us, as they did to Taylor, as 'the silent sentinels of the burial fires of a bygone race'?

Moor Divock 5 NY 493222

A short walk through the bracken from circle 4 brings one to this ruined cairn circle, referred to as site *g* by the RCHM.[36] From the site, Moor Divock 4, the two boulders mentioned earlier, and the Kopstone are clearly visible to the south-south-east; they appear almost in line.

Three large standing stones are all that remains of a former circle. They stand within the western quadrant of a much-delapidated cairn of stones, in the inner area of which are several circular depressions, probably the result of excavation. The diameter of the mound is approximately 14 m; but this is difficult to determine accurately, as many of the stones have been scattered around, and the outer area is obscured by bracken. Taylor described it (somewhat anatomically inaptly) as a 'starfish' cairn, owing to three spoke-like projections of small stones radiating from the cairn;[34] these are now difficult to detect. He also mentioned that the stone circle had been ruined in about 1870. The site was excavated by Canon Simpson, sometime vicar of Shap. In the centre of the circle he found a collared urn containing ashes and burnt bone,[41] which definitely dates the circle to the early bronze age.

Taylor claimed that the best-preserved part of the stone avenue was to be seen extending for a distance of about 200 m to the north-west of circle 5 in the direction of White Raise. There are indeed a number of low stones in this area; but they do not form part of a discernible avenue, nor is there any evidence to suggest that they were artificially placed. There is now no trace of the four small circles mentioned by Taylor between circle 5 and White Raise.

The Cockpit NY 483222

From the junction of the trackway across Moor Divock and the footpath to Askham, the Cockpit is clearly visible 0.5 km (about ¼ mile) to the south-west. But beware! The poorly-defined path that leads to the circle crosses what Wainwright describes as 'positively the worst bog on any regular Lakeland path'.[42] It may be prudent for the sake of one's feet to make a detour around the north of the bog. The circle is much visited by walkers, for just beyond the circle a good path leads around Barton Fell to Howtown and Ullswater. To the south and south-east of the circle Moor Divock stretches bleakly away, while to the north is the more varied prospect of the distant fells.

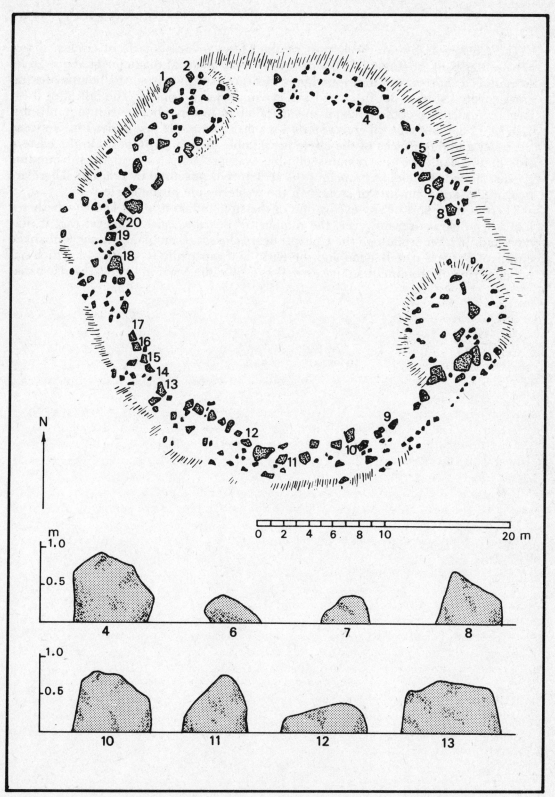

Fig. 4.12 The Cockpit, after Royal Commission on Historical Monuments (England).[43]

The Cockpit is by far the largest of the Moor Divock coterie of circles. A low penannular bank of stones, 3 m wide and with an internal diameter of about 26 m, surrounds a short-turfed interior which is featureless apart from the humps of a few grass-covered stones. Set into the bank are many larger stones. The tallest of these form the inner face of the circle; many are fallen or leaning, but several (notably nos. 4, 8, 10, 11 and 20) are still erect. Stone 4 reaches a height of just under 1 m. Between the inner and outer faces of the circle is a jumble of smaller stones. On the eastern side of the bank are the remains of what was probably a cairn; its surrounding circular bank is visible, but much of the structure is obscured by bracken. There are two similar arrangements of stones on the western side of the circle.

There is no report of any excavation of the site, and so it is not known whether it had a sepulchral use; however, the remains of possible cairns suggest that it may have had. In its morphology the Cockpit bears closest resemblance to the embanked circles of Furness (the Beacon and the Kirk) and especially to Casterton, which has an inner ring of prominent stones as well as a possible cairn in its penannular bank.

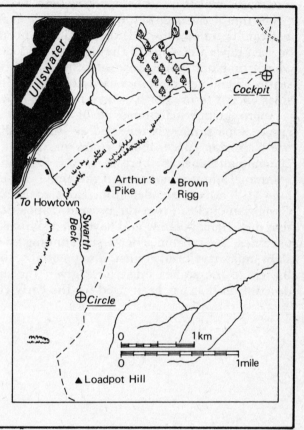

Swarth Fell

Location: NY 457192
On Swarth Fell
1.4 km (⅞ mile) ESE of Howtown
555 m above sea-level

This, the most isolated of all the Cumbrian stone circles, is 1 km (⅝ mile) to the north of the summit of Loadpot Hill. Two approaches are possible: there is a fairly steep ascent from Howtown on the shore of Ullswater, or a more leisurely, but longer, walk from the Cockpit – a distance of 4 km (2½ miles). The way from the Cockpit is along the course of High Street, the Roman road from Kendal to Penrith; but little trace of the Roman way now exists, and at best it is a rutted grass track. If this route is chosen, leave the Cockpit by the clearly-defined path to Howtown. High Street leaves this path to the left about 270 m beyond the circle. The way here is indistinct; but the correct course can be easily followed by heading for the summit of Loadpot Hill (the pillar on the top is clearly visible), and keeping well to the left of craggy Arthur's Pike. The path becomes very clear beyond an intermediate hill, and it can then be followed with ease.

The magnificent views obtained on the ascent in themselves justify the climb. Revealed to the west, during the upper stages of the walk, is a spectacularly intimate panorama of mountain scenery; the high Lakeland Fells, from the distant Coniston Old Man in the south to Skiddaw and Blencathra in the north, merge one into the other. Under a cumulus-clouded sky, the contrast of light and shadow on the mountains makes a most impressive and awe-inspiring sight.

The tumbled stones of the ring are at the head of a valley occupied by Swarth Beck, a stream that flows towards the north and north-west into Ullswater. The stones can be seen down the slope to the right of the footpath. The circle's location is unusual when compared with those of other Cumbrian stone circles: it is 550 m above sea-level, and was built in a natural hollow at the head of a gill. The land rises on all sides except to the north, where it slopes down the valley.

Approximately 65 stones, all of which have fallen, are what now remains of the circle. (One stone was reported as still standing in 1936.[44]) They are set round an open circular space about 16 m in diameter, and there is no indication of a penannular bank as there is at the Cockpit. Stones are absent in the western quadrant, and it is not clear if the circle was ever complete. Many of the stones are long (1-2 m) yet slender from front to back – again an unusual feature among Cumbrian circles. From the present disposition of the stone slabs, it would appear that the original plan would have been similar to that of the Cockpit, i.e. an annulus of stones, several stones deep, surrounding an open inner area. When erect the inner slabs must have been almost, if not actually, touching; and when viewed from within the circle the stones must have given the impression of a continuous fence – a description that has been used for the early circles of Swinside and Castlerigg.[45]

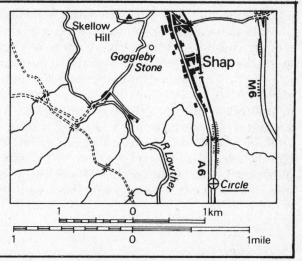

Kemp Howe

Location: NY 568133
2 km (1¼ miles) south of Shap
265 m above sea-level

The tumbled remains of Kemp Howe lie in a pasture-field by the eastern side of the A6, 2.5 km (1½ miles) south of Shap village. Six huge boulders of Shap granite, the largest being 3 m long, and several smaller stones lie fallen beneath the railway embankment, which destroyed the circle when the railway was built in the middle of the 19th century. The site of the circle is on level ground 700 m east of the river Lowther. Pennant, writing in 1769, described Kemp Howe as a 'large circle'.[46] If the remaining stones are typical of the other members of the circle, it must have been an impressive monument. The stones now form a flattened arc about 25 m across, a value that is close to the supposed original diameter of the circle (80 ft., 24.4 m).[47]

The real significance of the circle is that it seems to have formed the southern terminus of an avenue of standing stones called Shap Stones by some authors and Carls Lofts by others. (The latter name is now used for a terrace of houses in the main street of Shap.) The avenue went northwards from Kemp Howe towards Shap and then turned to the north-west, seemingly terminating at Skellaw Hill, on the top of which was a tumulus. The total length of the avenue would have been about 2.5 km. Recent work by Clare[48] has suggested that the avenue may have turned to avoid the tumulus on Skellaw Hill, and then progressed a further 600 m or so in a north-westerly direction. Local legend even claims that the avenue continued to Kop Stone on Moor Divock,[38] but there is certainly no evidence for this.

Pennant states that the width of the avenue was 88 ft. (27 m) in the south, but that the sides converged as the avenue progressed northwards, and the width was 59 ft. (18 m) as it passed Shap village.[46] Even at that time many of the stones had been lost by blasting to clear the land, and further mutilation continued throughout the 18th and 19th centuries. Nicolson and Burn, writing a few years after Pennant, reported that stones had been carried away for foundations of buildings and for use as millstones; and they added the recommendation that 'when polished they would make fine chimney pieces'.[49] Enclosure of the land in the early 19th century led to further destruction of the avenue in the southern part;[50] and as stated earlier, the construction of the railway toppled the southern terminus of Kemp Howe.

Yet some stones still remain; Clare's survey revealed 27 possible survivors.[48] The finest of them is the Goggleby Stone (see plate 16), a 2.2 m high slab of Shap granite tapering slightly down its length; there is a cup mark on its north-east angle. Clare found the stone fallen; so he took the opportunity to excavate beneath and re-erect it, and his findings reveal how the megalith-builders may have raised this and other stones. A socket hole was dug and a layer of clay placed at the bottom; then the monolith was slid into the hole and pulled upright. The clay provided temporary support while the monolith was wedged in position with packing stones.

There is little on which to base an estimate of the age of the avenue and Kemp Howe circle. Clare favours a late neolithic date,[48] in line with the late neolithic dates proposed for the stone avenues of south-west England and of Kennet Avenue, which links the great circle-henge of Avebury with the Sanctuary.

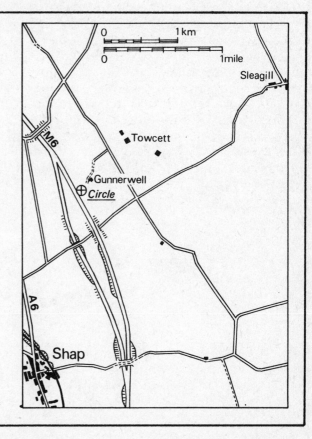

Gunnerkeld

Location: NY 568178
2.5 km (1½ miles) NNE of Shap
265 m above sea-level

To the north and east of Shap, the M6 motorway climbs along a valley towards Shap Summit on Hardendale Fell to the south. The builders of the Gunnerkeld circle chose this valley to raise their stones. Traffic now speeds past a few metres away from the circle, and four millenia of quiet enjoyed by the stones are ended. Yet the presence of the motorway gives the site that fascinating juxtaposition of ancient and modern technology that is so evident at Grey Croft. A motorist travelling south down the M6 can obtain a particularly good, if fleeting, view of the circle. This is an impressive site, and is well worth a visit. It is easily reached from the minor road from Strickland to Castlehowe, and involves a short walk along the track to Gunnerwell Farm. The name 'Gunnerkeld' apparently means 'sportsman's spring'.

The circle is built on a level limestone terrace in pasture-land. The valley sides rise gently to the east and west. It is an interesting monument, for it is in fact two concentric stone circles and combines the features of a great, open stone circle and a cairn circle. An outer megalithic ring surrounds a ring of smaller stones, which is itself built around a low burial mound. The plan of Gunnerkeld shown in fig. 4.13 is adapted from that produced by C. W. Dymond in the 1870s.[51] He found the seats of

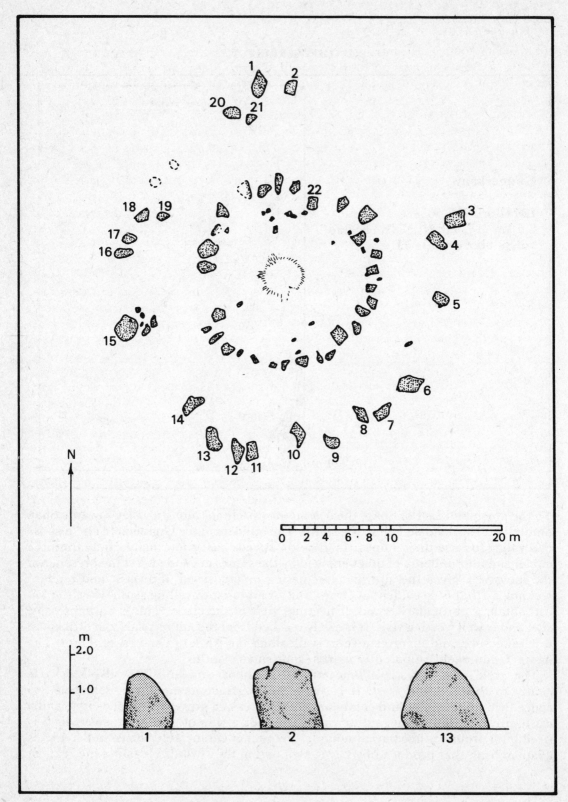

Fig. 4.13 Gunnerkeld, after Dymond.[51]

two missing stones in the north-west sector of the outer circle, and he concluded that eight to 10 stones in all had been removed. Three stones not shown in Dymond's original plan (nos. 17, 19 and 21) are shown in fig. 4.13; it is possible that these are recent additions to the ring and are not part of the original. The stones used in the construction of the rings are mainly Carboniferous limestone and granite.

All but three of the stones of the outer ring, nos. 1, 2 and 13, are now fallen. Stones 1 and 2 are due north of the centre and form what appears to be a portal. The similarity between this outer ring and the Carles, Castlerigg is quite remarkable: both are elongated towards the north, and their dimensions are almost identical (the north-south and east-west diameters are 31.8 m and 29.1 m at Gunnerkeld and 32.6 m and 29.5 m at the Carles); the sizes of the stones are similar in each; and in both circles two of the tallest stones are set at the north, one each side of the north-south axis, with a corresponding tall stone (no. 13 at Gunnerkeld) near the opposite point on the perimeter. The northern pair of stones at the Carles are claimed to form an entrance, and those at Gunnerkeld may do so as well. Are these similarities merely coincidences, or do they indicate a close connection between the Carles and the outer ring at Gunnerkeld? Were they perhaps built to the same 'megalithic architect's' plan? An argument against such a connection would be the age of Gunnerkeld, if it is assumed that the outer ring is contemporary with the central burial mound. The mound probably belongs to the early bronze age, whereas the Carles was built in the neolithic period. But at Gunnerkeld, we may again have a site that was modified some time after its construction. The sequence of events may have been as follows. An open stone circle was built in later neolithic times mainly for ceremonial and ritual use, as was the Carles. When social customs changed during the early bronze age, the circle was altered to fulfil a sepulchral use, and the central mound and its surrounding stone circle were inserted.

The stones of the inner ring are mostly smaller than those of the outer. All but one (no. 22) are prostrate, and many are in danger of being hidden beneath the turf. In the northern part of the ring is a roughly circular arrangement of low stones. The inner ring is also slightly elongated (15.8 m north to south and 14.6 m east to west). The low central mound, which reaches to the stones of the inner ring, has a depression in the centre, and the remains of a burial cist are visible; but what the cist contained is unfortunately not recorded.

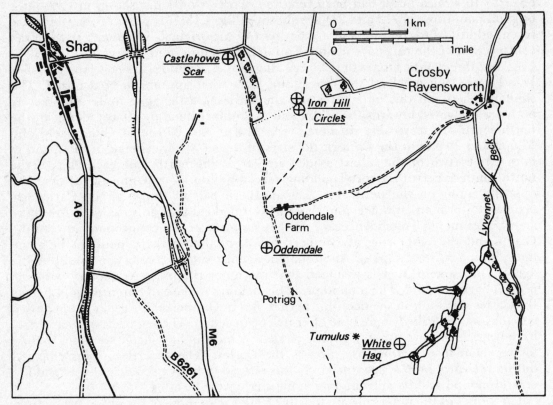

Fig. 4.14 Location of the Crosby Ravensworth circles.

Between Shap and Crosby Ravensworth an area of Carboniferous limestone forms the Hardendale and Crosby Ravensworth Fells. Like the limestone country around Great Urswick, in the far south of Cumbria, there is much evidence of prehistoric activity. There are many burial mounds, mainly belonging to the bronze age, and several of these are in prominent positions on or near hill tops. Remains of a number of early settlements can be found on the hills. One of these is the important Romano-British settlement of Ewe Close, 1.5 km (1 mile) to the south-west of Crosby Ravensworth; it lies beside the Roman road from Lancaster to Carlisle. The Ewe Close site bears many similarities to the Romano-British settlement of Urswick Stone Walls (p. 35).

The limestone hills are dotted with ice-borne boulders of Shap granite, and it is these that early bronze age people used in the construction of the stone circles of the area. The five circles (or six, if the tiny companion of Oddendale is included) lie roughly in a line from Castlehowe Scar in the north-west to White Hag in the south-east; and they are all accessible from the trackway that runs from Castlehowe to Oddendale Farm and beyond onto Crosby Ravensworth Fell.

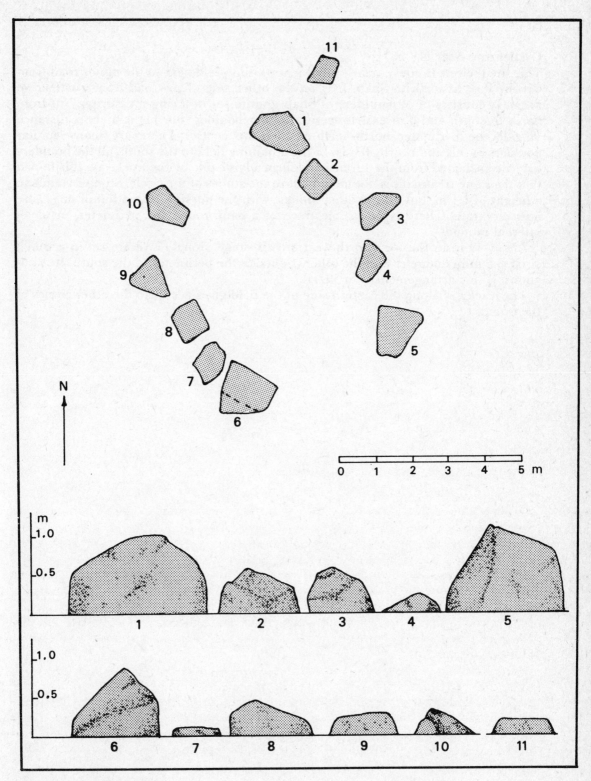

Fig. 4.15 Castlehowe Scar.

Castlehowe Scar NY 587154

This small circle is conveniently sited in a pasture-field next to the minor road from Crosby Ravensworth to Shap. It is on the other side of the road from Castlehowe Farm. It consists of 10 boulders of Shap granite set in a ring measuring 7 m from north to south and 6 m east to west. Another boulder (no. 11) is a short distance outside the perimeter north-north-east of the centre. There are many similar boulders in this and nearby fields. In the adjoining field to the south, all the boulders have been cleared from the surface and form a large pile by the trackway. It is hoped that the same treatment is not meted out to the stones of the circle. Stone 5 stands to a height of 1.1 m, but all the other stones, with the possible exception of no. 1, are now prostrate. There is no visible trace of a bank round the perimeter, or of an internal mound.

About 33 m to the west-north-west are six small stones. Five are set in a rough circle 3.5 m in diameter and the other is outside the perimeter to the south. It is not known if this arrangement is artificial.

The trackway along the eastern side of the field gives access to the other circles of the group.

The Iron Hill Circles

The trackway runs along the side of a woods for the first km (½ mile); and at the southern edge of the woods a path leaves the track and leads up the hill to the two circles at the top. The smaller of the two (the southern one) is clearly visible from the trackway below. The northern circle, some 60 m from its companion, is set on the highest point of the flat-topped hill. The positions of the circles may well have been chosen to make them conspicuous at a distance, and also for the uninterrupted views in all directions from the top of the hill. To the west, beyond an imposing cement works, are the Lakeland Fells; the regular outlines of the Howgill Fells form the southern horizon; to the east, across the pastoral Eden valley, is the dark wall of the Pennines; in the far distance to the north are the Cheviots. This certainly would have made a fine resting-place for a man of stature in his community, disturbed now only by the grazing sheep and in the early summer by the unexpected, anxious cries of nesting oyster catchers.

Iron Hill North NY 596148

Nineteen low boulders surround the base of a mound about 1 m high in the centre. The stones are set close together in the south, but they are more widely spaced in the north and east. It may be that stones in this sector have been removed, and that the mound was originally surrounded by a continuous kerb of stones. The stones are variously Shap granite, limestone and a dark igneous rock. The largest is no. 1, measuring 1.75 m by 1.2 m round its base and 75 cm high. A stone wall bisects the circle and mound, and this makes it difficult to get an overall impression of the site. Access from one half to the other is best made through a gate in the wall, a short distance to the east.

Thom has classed Iron Hill North as a flattened circle Type D;[13] it measures 14.5 m from north to south and 11.5 m from east to west. He calls the circle Haberwain, after the farmhouse 1 km (⅝ mile) to the east.

Iron Hill South NY 596147

A short distance across the short turf from the northern circle, and slightly down the hill, is the stone circle of Iron Hill South. Nine stones form a ring around the top of a low mound. Stone 2 is 2-3 m outside the perimeter, a feature reminiscent of Castlehowe Scar. Three other stones, which may be the remains of a cist, occupy the hollowed centre of the mound. The site falls within Lynch's definition of a cairn circle (p. 14). The stones of the circle are very prominent; the tallest, no. 4, is just over 1 m high; and all the stones, apart from no. 6, are Shap granite. Thom classifies the shape as an ellipse, and quotes its axes as being 8.5 MY and 7.5 MY (7.1 m by 6.2 m).[52]

In the mid-19th century Simpson reported the 'careless' excavation of the circle which took place some years earlier.[38] The bones of a 'man of great stature', and portions of deer antler 'much larger than those of our days' and other animal bones are all that is recorded of the discoveries.

133

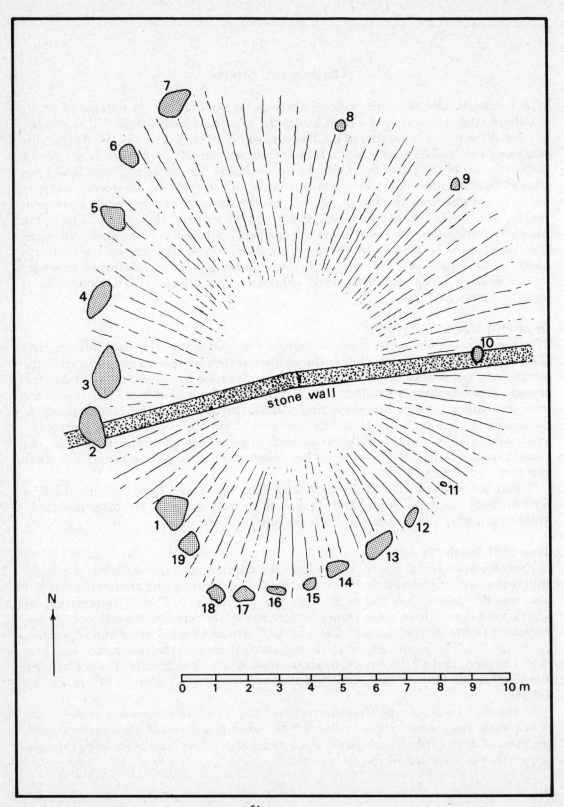

Fig. 4.16 Iron Hill North, after Collingwood.[54]

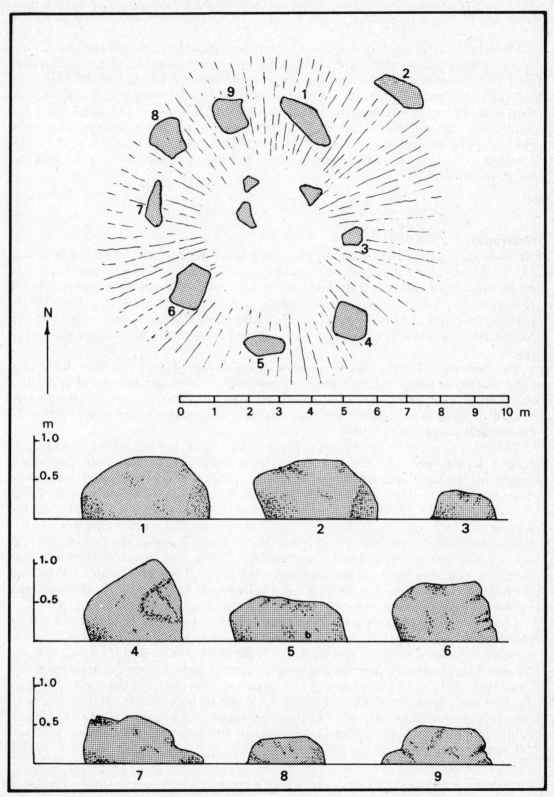

Fig. 4.17   Iron Hill South, after Collingwood.[54]

There is virtually no evidence that suggests a relationship between the two circles, apart from their proximity; but it is likely that they share a common relationship with the other bronze age burial mounds on or near the summits of nearby hills. One such site is the now-ruined tumulus of Penhurrock (NY 629104), on the side of the minor road from Orton to Crosby Ravensworth. This site has been used as a quarry for road-stone, and all that remains are a denuded mound and a number of granite boulders. The mound was originally surrounded by a circle of granite boulders (the remaining ones may have belonged to this), and human bones were found in a cist under the mound.[41, 53]

Oddendale NY 592129

An ill-defined path passes through the gate a short distance to the east of Iron Hill North. It leads along the elongated top of Iron Hill and eventually brings the walker to the hamlet of Oddendale, after which the finest of the Crosby Ravensworth circles is named. In 19th-century texts the name is sometimes rendered 'Odendale' or, perhaps revealing the origin of the name, 'Odindale'. The site of the circle is on the local summit of a low hill, on which a limestone pavement shows through the turf in places.

The Oddendale circle consists of two concentric rings of stones, as does the nearby Gunnerkeld, to which it bears some resemblance. Oddendale is somewhat smaller than Gunnerkeld, however, and its stones are lower and less impressive; also the two concentric rings at Oddendale are almost perfect concentric circles, whereas those of Gunnerkeld are more irregular.

The outer circle of 34 stones has a diameter of 27.1 m, but the tallest stone (no. 7) is only 64 cm high. Several stones lie in a band outside the main perimeter, suggesting an annular arrangement of stones rather than a simple circle. As in the other circles in the area, most of the stones are Shap granite. The inner circle, 7.4 m in diameter, forms a kerb of almost contiguous stones around a low mound, on the surface of which are several large stones. The stones of the inner ring are smaller than those of the outer, the tallest being 40 cm high. Towards the end of the 19th century, the central mound was excavated by Canon Simpson. His laconic report mentions that only traces of burnt matter were found,[41] but presumably the mound did hold an early bronze age burial. R. G. Collingwood has pointed out the similarity between the mound and inner circle here and the northern Iron Hill circle.[54]

Close to the outer circle are several large granite stones, notably three prostrate boulders a few metres to the north-east; but on superficial inspection it is not possible to know if they are connected with the circle. They could, for example, be displaced stones of the outer circle. One definite structure outside the main circle is a small ring of 11 low or buried stones 22.5 m north of the centre of the circle. This tiny satellite has a diameter of only 4.3 m (fig. 4.18) and its highest stone stands a mere 10 cm above the turf. The only other intimate association of a large and small circle still extant in Cumbria is the Lacra D complex (p. 49), although Castlehowe Scar and White Hag may have smaller companions.

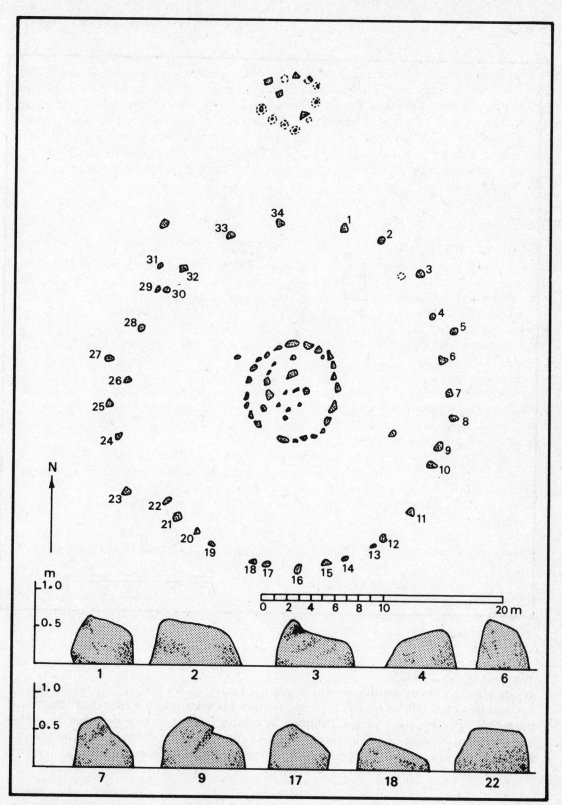

Fig. 4.18 Oddendale.

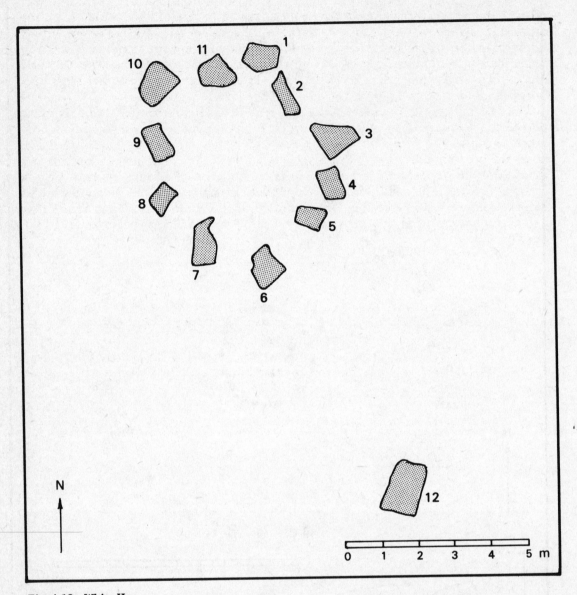

Fig. 4.19   White Hag.

White Hag NY 607116

White Hag, the most southerly of this group of circles, lies 350 m east-south-east of the summit of a hill on which a tumulus rises above a much-weathered limestone pavement. The position of the tumulus is clearly indicated at a distance by a tall wooden post set within it. The post bears an official notice declaring the tumulus to be a national monument. A level patch of land on the hillside was chosen as the site of the circle. The land slopes down to the south to Lyvennet Beck, which is on the other side of a sparse woods. A few metres to the south of the circle is a drystone wall bordering the woods, and 25 m to the south is a conspicuous tumulus. There are many granite boulders scattered around the hillside; four are set close together in a rectangular arrangement 9 m to the north-west of the circle, and another large one, possibly an outlier, is 9.5 m to the south of the circle.

The 11 Shap granite boulders of the circle, all now fallen, surround a central space devoid of a mound or any other structure. It is a very small circle, slightly elongated north to south, and with a north-south diameter of 6 m. White Hag and Castlehowe Scar are very similar: they resemble each other in size and in the number and disposition of stones, and they also show no evidence of an embankment or any internal feature. The small circle at Oddendale is of like size, but its stones are of almost insignificant height. The only other circle in Cumbria similar to White Hag and Castlehowe Scar is the small, seven-stoned circle on Bleaberry Haws, far to the west (p. 39).

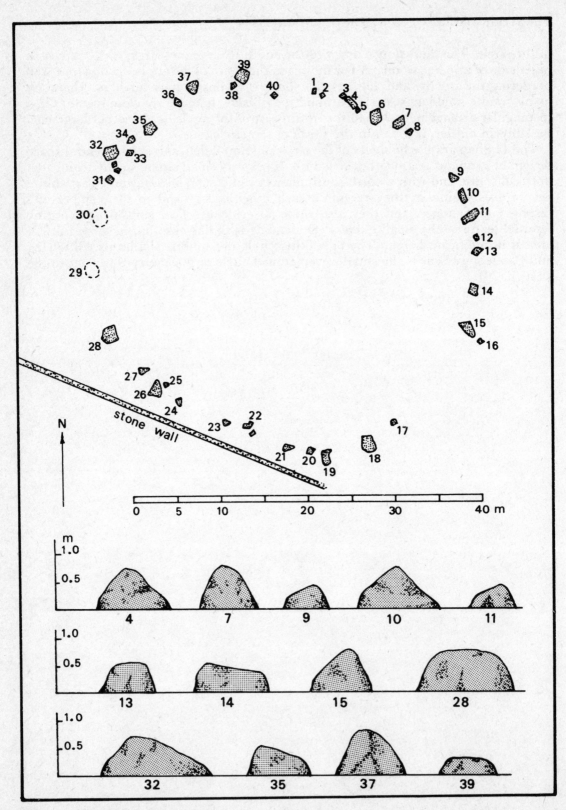

Fig. 4.20 Gamelands.

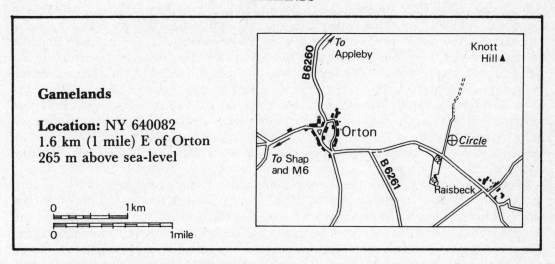

Gamelands

Location: NY 640082
1.6 km (1 mile) E of Orton
265 m above sea-level

On low land below Knott Hill just to the east of Orton is the great stone circle of Gamelands. It is a large circle, one of the largest in Cumbria, but all of its stones are tumbled. None now attains a height of 1 m, and the circle must have lost much of its former visual impact. Unlike the well-known great circles of the Carles and Long Meg and her Daughters, it is infrequently visited, even though access to it is very easy. It is a few metres east of the trackway that runs northwards from the Orton to Raisbeck road over the western flank of Knott Hill. The stone-walled field in which the circle lies is private farm land and is used as a meadow.

About forty stones remain (see plate 19). It is difficult to tell if some of the smaller ones are spurious or if they are the blasted remnants of larger stones. It is an elongated ring (flattened circle Type A according to Thom,[13] who refers to the circle as Orton), measuring 44.4 m from east to west and 38.8 m from north to south. All the stones are Shap granite with the exception of no. 19, which is limestone. Careful inspection shows that the stones are set in a low bank. This has led to the circle's being compared with the Druids' Circle at Penmaenmawr in Gwynedd, N. Wales.[55, 56] At this latter site the stones of a circle of diameter 25 m are set around the inner face of a circular rubble bank which is up to 0.5 m high. The bank at Gamelands is much less impressive than this; and under the long grass of early summer it is virtually invisible. The bank seems more similar to the residual low bank in the western sector of Long Meg and her Daughters. Gamelands, however, is the only complete example in Cumbria of an embanked stone circle (fig. 2.1c).

The circle is built on land that is not entirely flat. From the centre of the circle the land slopes up gently to the south, before falling away again beyond the stone wall that almost touches the southern stones of the circle. These southern stones are therefore on noticeably higher land than the rest. The gap in the south-east sector, between stones 21 and 22, is possibly an entrance; it overlooks land that falls away to the south-east.

Ferguson reported that the land was first ploughed in or around 1863.[57] The plough was taken right through the circle; and to facilitate the operation, two or three stones were buried by being rolled into pits dug under them (stones 8 and 9 may be these), and one or two others were broken up by blasting. It is fortunate that the farmer did not carry out any further modifications. The ploughing disturbed the central area and revealed a sandstone slab, possibly the cover of a burial cist. In the original survey of the circle, carried out in 1880, the slab is shown by stone 29, but is has since disappeared. No other evidence for an interment within the circle was discovered, and the only other finds were two pieces of worked flint.[57] In the absence of a proper excavation one should not draw too many conclusions, but such paucity of finds is typical of the large, open stone circles belonging to the later neolithic period.

Finally, a footnote about the name 'Gamelands'. Games were held until the 19th century at the Kirk circle on Kirkby Moor and at King Arthur's Round Table, but there is no evidence that Gamelands was used in this way; so the name is unlikely to derive from activities of this type. Ferguson has suggested that the name refers to the surrounding land, which may originally have been called Gamesland after Gramel-de-Pennington, first lord of Orton.[57] An alternative view has it that the name simply signifies that the land was used for cattle – 'Gamp(us)land'.[41]

Hird Wood

Location: NY 417059
On the side of Hird Gill
4 km (2½ miles) NE of Ambleside
230 m above sea-level

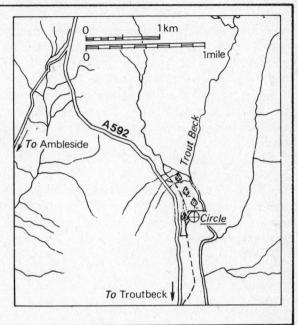

North of Troutbeck the A592 climbs up and along the steep-sided valley of Trout Beck towards the Kirkstone Pass. The Hird Wood circle, isolated and ruined, lies just to the east of the road 3 km (2 miles) north of Troutbeck. The road is fairly featureless here, and the way to the circle is not obvious. The way is marked by a gate in the stone wall on the east side of the road about 200 m past a ruined building with stepped gables. A rough track leads from the gate down the valley side and merges into a rather overgrown ancient trackway known as Low Kingate, so named in contrast to High Kingate, now the A592. Low Kingate passes through a wood for a short distance until it meets a ruined gateway, beyond which is an area of open land. The circle is just through the gateway.

The situation of the circle is unusual. It is built on a fairly level but narrow shoulder of land on the steep side of Trout Beck valley. The land rises abruptly to the west and falls to the east, to rise steeply again on the other side of Trout Beck. The whole effect is rather claustrophobic, especially when compared with the panoramic views obtained from the sites of other stone circles.

The circle is very delapidated, partly because Low Kingate goes through it, and its original form is difficult to make out. Its existence was first recorded in 1934,[58] when it was described as consisting of two concentric circles of total diameter 65 ft. (19.8 m). The tallest remaining stone, no. 6, is 1.1 m high. This, together with several smaller and tumbled stones, seems to belong to the inner ring, although the boundary of this ring is difficult to discern. The outer ring is even more obscure. Three large stones in the base of the stone wall (nos. 8, 9 and 10) may have been

143

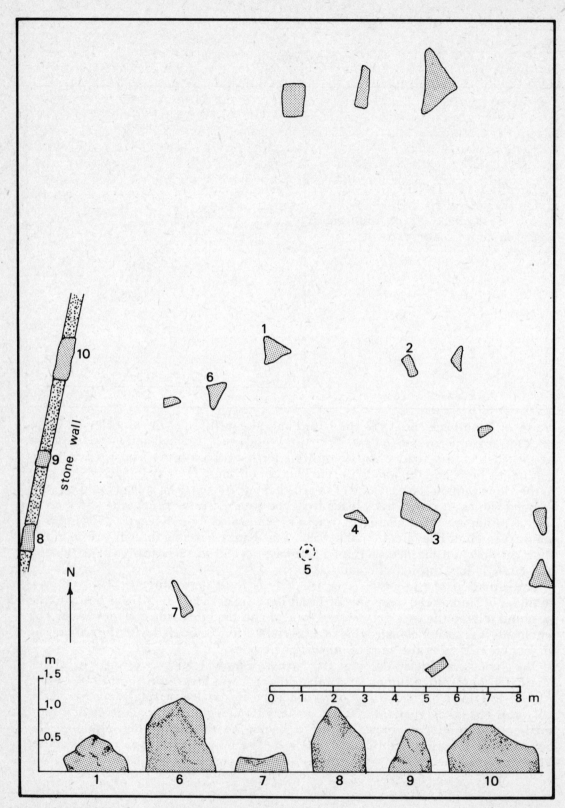

Fig. 4.21 Hird Wood.

members of it, as may the group of three large stones to the north (fig. 4.21); but there are several large stones scattered around the area, and it is impossible to know which, if any, belong to the circle. One definite feature of the circle is the rise in ground level towards the centre, and this may indicate the presence of a burial mound within the circle. It is possible that the site resembled the Druids' Circle on Birkrigg, and a burial mound would suggest an early bronze age date. However, a roughed-out Cumbrian-type stone axe was apparently found about 55 m to the south in a pile of stones removed from the circle.[58] If the axe were indeed associated with the circle, this would imply an earlier date for activity on the site. But with so little evidence, it would be rash to make any firm suggestion for the site's age and original nature.

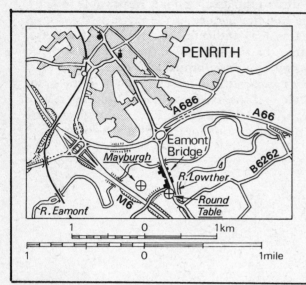

Mayburgh

Location: NY 519284
120 m above sea-level

King Arthur's Round Table

Location: NY 523283
130 m above sea-level
Both are 2 km (1¼ miles) S of Penrith

Mayburgh

Mayburgh, a Class I henge (fig. 2.2a), is on a tongue of land between the river Eamont (250 m to the north-west) and the river Lowther (500 m to the east) just to the south of Penrith.

It consists of a single circular bank, up to 6.4 m high and 50 m across its base, which encloses an area having an average diameter of around 87 m. Due east of the centre of the henge is an entrance in the bank about 3 m wide, and beyond the entrance the land slopes down to the river Lowther. It is unusual for the bank of a henge to have no accompanying ditch; but the absence of a ditch at Mayburgh results from its method of construction. For most henges the material excavated from the ditch was used to build the bank. At Mayburgh, however, the bank is composed entirely of cobbles brought from the beds of the two nearby rivers. Dymond estimated that the work involved in building the bank would have fully occupied 1000 men for 6 months or longer.[59]

The inner area is now featureless, apart from a single monolith 2.8 m high (see plate 21), which presides alone over the empty inner space. It is likely, however, that it once belonged to a circle of standing stones within the henge. Pennant's plan of Mayburgh (fig. 4.22b), published in 1769,[60] shows the positions of four other stones of this circle, three of which had by that time disappeared. His plan also shows the positions of two pairs of standing stones flanking each side of the elongated entrance (fig. 4.22b). Stukeley, writing of his visit to Mayburgh in 1725, records the former existence of not one, but two circles of 'huge stones' within the henge.[61] The diameter of the inner circle is given as 50 ft. (about 15 m). But even when Stukeley saw the site, little remained of the stone circles. The inner area had been ploughed a few years previously, and this must have led to the removal of most of the stones. On the evidence available, it seems reasonable to assume that Mayburgh originally

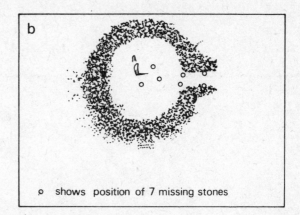

shows position of 7 missing stones

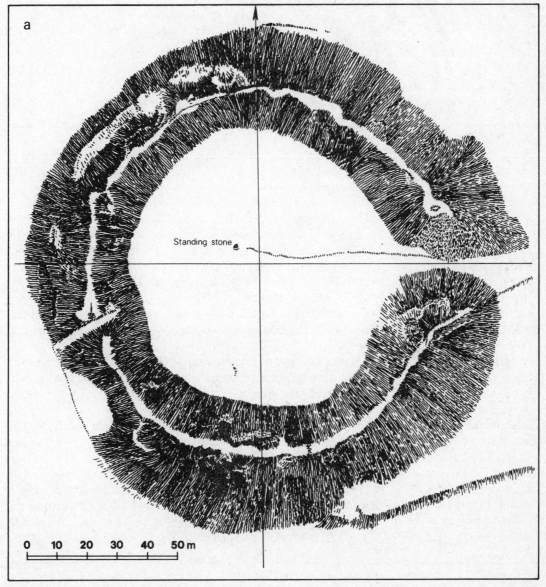

Standing stone

0 10 20 30 40 50 m

Fig. 4.22 Mayburgh: a) Present day appearance (after Dymond[59]); b) Pennant's sketch of Mayburgh in 1769.[60]

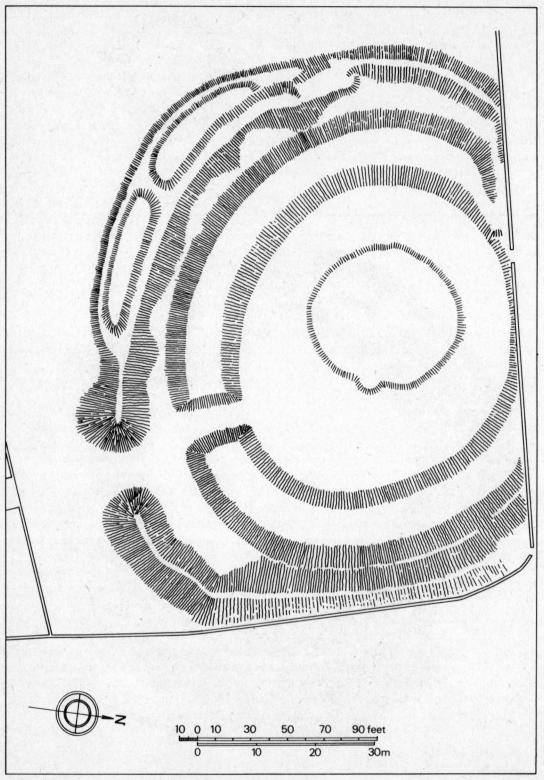

Fig. 4.23 King Arthur's Round Table, after Collingwood.[64]

contained at least one stone circle, and it can therefore be classed as a circle-henge (fig. 2.2c).

The only finds reported from the monument are a 'brass celt' (bronze axe) found during ploughing[61] and a broken roughed-out stone axe found in the entrance.[62]

Can anything be said about its age and relationship with the Cumbrian stone circles? The bank encloses an area similar in size to the stones of the Long Meg circle; and the porch-like arrangement of stones in Pennant's plan is remarkably similar to the entrances of the early circles of Long Meg and Swinside, which belong to the later neolithic period. Further evidence for a similar early date for Mayburgh is provided by the roughed-out stone axe found there, and also by its position on one of the proposed trade routes for the transport of stone axes (fig. 2.8). The radiocarbon dates available suggest that the first henges were being built at the same time as, or perhaps somewhat earlier than, the earliest stone circles. Whether Mayburgh was a forerunner of the early Cumbrian stone circles, or whether it represents a fusion of the stone circle tradition of Cumbria and an intrusive henge tradition, is a matter for debate.

King Arthur's Round Table (see plate 20)

Although King Arthur's Round Table does not possess a stone circle, nor probably ever possessed one, it would be an obvious omission not to include this well-known but much-mutilated henge, especially as it is only 350 m east of the circle-henge of Mayburgh. It stands in the corner of a field in Eamont Bridge, at the junction of the A6 and the minor road to Sockbridge.

The impressive earthwork consists of an irregular bank surrounding a circular ditch which is 12 m wide and 1.2 to 1.5 m deep. There is an entrance in the bank in the south-east, and this leads to a causeway across the ditch, although the causeway and ditch are not quite in line. The bank reaches its greatest height of 2 m at the entrance, and is about 12 m wide here. In the western sector there is a berm – a level strip – 4 to 6 m wide between the bank and the ditch, but this is absent in the east. The enclosures that have been set into the bank in the south and south-west are of relatively recent date. The ditch surrounds a roughly circular platform varying from 52 to 44 m in diameter. The raised circular disc within the central area is also comparatively recent.

Towards the end of the 19th century the bank and ditch in the north were destroyed when the road to Sockbridge was constructed.[59] The bank in the east has also been partially removed by the widening of the A6. There was, originally, an entrance in the bank at the north-west, opposite the present one: this would make the Round Table a Class II henge (fig. 2.2b). A plan drawn by Stukeley in the first half of the 18th century[61] shows the Round Table with its second entrance. Before this time two large stones apparently stood outside the destroyed entrance. They are shown on a drawing made by Sir William Dugdale in the 16th century,[63] and they are also mentioned by Aubrey in his 'Monumenta Britannia'. The stones had disappeared by the time Stukeley visited the site some seventy or so years after Aubrey. There is clearly a possibility that there were more than two standing stones in or around the monument originally.

Substantial alterations were carried out in about 1820 by William Bushby, who owned the public house just across the road.[59] He turned the henge into a tea-garden; and to effect the transformation he raised the central platform by depositing on it over 1000 cu. metres of stone and gravel. He obtained much of the material by cutting away the inner face of the bank, producing the present steep-scarped inner face and also possibly the berm in the south and west. He raised the 'disc' above the level of the central platform, and he deepened the ditch.

Excavations were conducted here in 1937 by R. G. Collingwood[64] and a year or so later by Bersu.[63] They were able to trace the 'improvements' carried out by Bushby, and quantities of early 19th-century pottery were found, the results of its use as a tea-garden. However, they discovered little relating to the original use of the monument. The only certain prehistoric feature found in the central area was a hollow which Collingwood termed a 'cremation trench'.[64] This lay on the east side of the central platform, and it contained cremated bone and fragments of hazel charcoal. It was evident, however, that the body was cremated elsewhere and the remains buried in the trench. Large stones lay scattered around, and these may have formed a cairn over the burial. The feature had been much disturbed during the remodelling of the platform, and little information could be gained from it. During the excavation it was discovered that the entrance had been widened towards the east and the causeway had been narrowed from the east, perhaps by Bushby. It was clear that in the first instance the entrance and causeway would have been in line.

From the results of the excavations and the historical descriptions, the original form of the henge can be reconstructed. A flat-topped bank about 10 m wide and 1.5 m high surrounded the ditch, with no intervening berm. There were two entrances opposite each other and two causeways, all of which were on the same axis. Two stones (perhaps more?) stood outside the northern entrance. Perhaps initially, or maybe at some later date, a burial was placed in a trench in the central platform. The burial was covered by some sort of structure, probably a cairn, for which large blocks of stone were used.

There is no direct means of dating the site. It is believed that Class II henges were generally of later date than Class I henges; so it may be that King Arthur's Round Table is younger by several centuries or even longer than nearby Mayburgh, but there is no further evidence for this suggestion.

Before leaving the Round Table, it is worth mentioning another henge-like monument that once existed in the vicinity, but of which now only the merest trace remains. It was called the Little Round Table. In his book of 1769, Pennant shows the Little Round Table lying about 150 m south of King Arthur's Round Table.[60] Stukeley describes it as having a diameter of 300 ft. (about 90 m) and consisting of a low circular bank surrounded by a ditch.[65] All that can now be seen of the site is a slight hollow in the field to the south of the Round Table by the side of a small wood. A stone wall enclosing the wood has cut off most of the monument, and to the east of the wall no sign of it now remains. A brief excavation carried out by Bersu[63] showed that if this is the remains of the Little Round Table, the bank surrounded the ditch and not vice-versa as Stukeley described.

SOME VANISHED CIRCLES OF NORTH AND EAST CUMBRIA

Grey Yauds NY 545487

Of all the Cumbrian stone circles known to have been destroyed the greatest – and saddest – loss is Grey Yauds. (A yaud is a horse or jade.) This was a large circle of many tall stones, and possibly belonged to the earliest stage of circle-building in Cumbria. Nicolson and Burn, in their 18th-century history of Cumberland, described the circle as consisting of 88 'pretty large' stones of granite forming a 'nearly exact circle' 52 yds (47.5 m) in diameter.[66] The tallest stones were 1.2 m to 1.5 m high,[67] and there was an outlier, taller than the other stones, about 5 m to the north-east.[68] By the second half of the 19th century the numbers of stones had been reduced by the 'necessities of agriculture';[67] the stones were used to build walls when the common was enclosed;[69] and now only the solitary outlier remains. There is a report of a more distant outlier, split in two,[70] but there is now no sign of this.

The site of Grey Yauds is 220 m above sea-level on the eastern flank of a ridge of Triassic (St Bees) sandstone, which runs north to south between the river Eden, 3 km (2 miles) to the west, and the steep scarp of the Pennines, 2 km (1¼ miles) to the east. The highest point of the ridge is Lawson Hill (243 m), 1 km (⅝ mile) to the west of the site of the circle. The tract of land on which the circle was built is known as King Harry Moor, described by Hutchinson in the late 18th century as a 'dark and dreary waste'.[71] Local tradition claims that the name was given when one of the King Henrys camped here; but the name is more likely to be a corruption of 'Kynheure', the name applied to the area in a 13th-century document. The location has been described as being in a natural pass between the Eden and the Pennines.[72] This lends support to the notion that Grey Yauds, together with the other early stone circles, was linked with the trade in neolithic stone axes. The circle would have been on the route northwards, perhaps via the Mayburgh henge, from the factory and flaking sites in the central fells to the Solway lowlands and southern Scotland.

The outlier lies in a field that is now used as arable land. To the immediate west of the stone the land is reasonably flat, before climbing to a conifer plantation and Lawson Hill; and to the east is a mound in the field which hides the stone from the visitor climbing up the hillside from the road below. The outlier is a large block of granodiorite standing 1.78 m high and 1.3 m across its broad top. A local legend has it that King Harold, or according to some, King 'Harry', used the stone as a mounting-block – he must have had a very tall horse!

The vanished circle must have been on the level land just to the west of the outlier. A stone wall now runs across the field through this position, and at the base of the wall is the only material evidence for the circle's existence; for here are several large lumps of granite – the broken stones of the great circle.

Wilson Scar NY 550183

The spoil heaps of a large quarry now cover the site of this circle, which was 3 km (2 miles) north of Shap just to the west of the A6. Spence's plan of the circle (fig. 4.24), published in 1935, shows a perfect circle of 17 m diameter.[73] It was bisected by a drystone wall, a fate shared by several other Cumbrian circles. The stones were

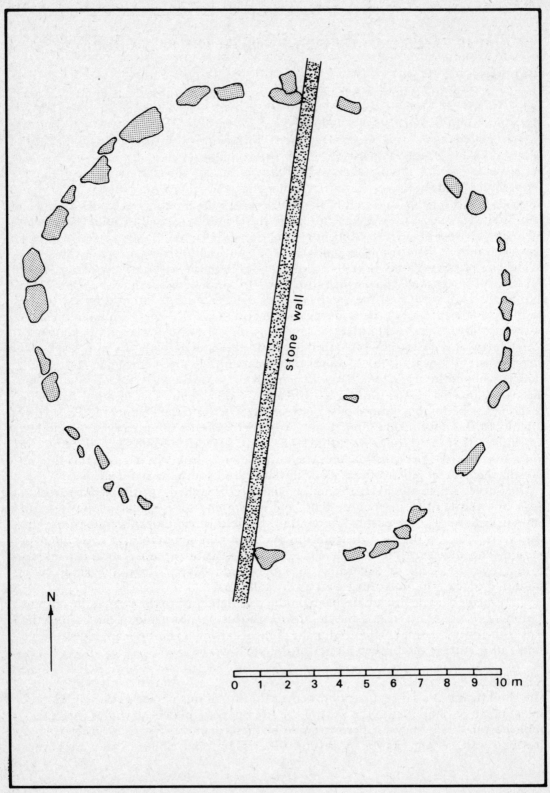

stone wall

N

0 1 2 3 4 5 6 7 8 9 10 m

Fig. 4.24   Wilson Scar, after Spence.[73]

glacial erratics of the Borrowdale Volcanic series, and they were probably collected locally as more of the same were scattered around the site. The stones of the circle were low, and the higher stones of the north-west sector only reached a height of 0.5 m. A rescue excavation was carried out here in 1952, with the help of boys from Penrith Queen Elizabeth School, just before the destruction of the circle by the quarry. A report of the dig was published in the *Cumberland and Westmorland Herald* on 20 December 1952.* The only find mentioned was a burial pit by one of the stones, containing charcoal and fragments of bone.

Brougham Hall

Brougham Hall is the name given to this obscure circle by Burl.[74] All that is known of the monument was recorded by Pennant in his 18th-century itinerary of northern England and Scotland.[75] He located the site opposite the circle-henge of Mayburgh on the other side of the river Eamont, which would now place it in the southern outskirts of Penrith. He described the site as a circle of large grit stones about 60 ft (18.2 m) in diameter surrounding a vast cairn of round stones.

Chapel Flat

This was the most northerly-known stone circle in Cumbria, but it has now completely vanished. It lay near the village of Dalston in the Carlisle lowlands near the river Caldew, 7 km (4½ miles) south-west of Carlisle. An 18th-century account[76] describes it as consisting of 'rude' stones 1 m in circumference set in a circle of diameter about 27 m. East of the centre of the circle were four large stones lying on top of each other. They may have been the remains of a cist, or possibly a tumbled cove, like that inside the circle-henge of Arbor Low in Derbyshire. A tumulus may have stood nearby.[77]

Broad Field NY 4345

Broad Field is a fairly flat area of land, 140-150 m above sea-level, to the east of Roe Beck (a tributary of the river Caldew) about 11 km (7 miles) to the south-south-east of Carlisle; it once formed part of Inglewood, a royal forest in medieval times. The site of the circle was about 1.5 km (1 mile) west of Broadfield House. A description of the monument written in the late 18th century[78] records that even then only six large stones remained; many other large stones had been blasted and carried away. The six stones were arranged in three pairs around the flat top of a low circular mound; the top of the mound was 63 ft. (19.2 m) in diameter. The circle was dug into in 1789, and three cists (described as stone chests) containing 'pieces of skull and bones' were found between the three pairs of stones and the centre of the circle.[78] There is also a suggestion in the same account that the circle once had an avenue of stones leading to it; for a number of large stones lay 50 m to the south of the circle, and others had apparently been blasted and removed to help ploughing.

---

*A full excavation report has now been published in *Transactions of the Cumberland and Westmorland Antiquarian and Archaeological Society*, 1984, vol. 84, p. 31. Apart from the cremation mentioned above, two inhumations and a second cremation were also found, along with traces of what may have been a paved area.

Motherby NY 419282

This stone circle stood 1 km (⅝ mile) to the west of the village of Motherby, just to the north of the A66 mid-way between Penrith and Keswick. Its diameter was about 15.5 m, and it was destroyed by blasting by the steward of the Duke of Norfolk in the first half of the 19th century[4] – a fate that it shares with the Lamplugh circle. W. G. Collingwood, writing in 1923, mentions the possibility that one stone remained.[79] The grid reference given above is that quoted by Burl,[80] and in fact there is a standing stone close to that position. It is about 1 m long and leaning slightly, and it stands on fairly level ground 150 m to the east of Skitwath Beck. It is not known for certain whether this is the stone mentioned by Collingwood; however, there are several large stones in the base of a destroyed stone wall a few metres to the south, and there is a pile of boulders at the bottom of the slope to the north-west. It is tempting to think that these stones are the remains of the circle of Motherby.

Rawthey Bridge

Little is known about this site. Nicolson and Burn[81] place it by the road from Kirkby Stephen to Sedbergh near Rawthey Bridge, i.e. just on the edge of the Howgill Fells. They describe it simply as a circle of large stones, supposed to be a monument of Druid worship.

Grasmere

This is another obscure site. It is given only a very brief mention by Hodgson in his history of Westmorland written in the early 19th century.[82] He describes it as consisting of several large stones standing near the point where the road from Keswick meets the road to Grasmere. Many of the stones had been displaced to make room for the roads. The original appearance of the site is, of course, unknown.

Knipe Scar NY 5319

Knipe Scar is an elevated area of limestone 5 km (3 miles) north-west of Shap. Simpson, writing in the middle of the 19th century, reported the presence of 3 sets of concentric stone circles on or near Knipe Scar.[41] One was found to contain charcoal and burnt earth. The exact locations of the circles were not given, and they appear no longer to exist.

Postscript

I have attempted in this book to include all known stone circles in Cumbria. It must be obvious, however, that such a task is virtually impossible; for the term 'stone circle' has no strict definition, and I have had to set what is in effect an arbitrary boundary to encompass the term. As has been shown, the term is limited to neolithic and early bronze age monuments; therefore the 18th-century stone circle folly on St Herbert's Island in Derwent Water is not included. Other sites that fall outside my own understanding of the term are some cairns marked on the Ordnance Survey maps as 'cairn circles' but which have little in common in terms of appearance with the cairn circles of north and east Cumbria. Such a site is the so-called Giant's Grave near Woodland in Furness (SD 256880). Also not included is the circle of boulders on the limestone pavement of Knipe Scar near Shap (NY 529193). This site is a circular enclosure about 15 m in diameter seemingly made by re-arranging some of the numerous blocks of limestone on the top of the hill. Although the site is labelled 'stone circle' on Ordnance Survey maps, it appears to be entirely different from the sorts of sites described in this book.

One interesting site, which I may have unfairly condemned to the end section, lies on Potter Fell, 6.5 km (4 miles) to the north of Kendal (SD 503988). Here, 19 or 20 low stones (the highest stands only 0.5 m above the turf) are set around an empty circular space about 20 m across. The site was reported in 1960 by Plint,[1] who assumed it to be a prehistoric stone circle. It has, however, been dismissed as a cockpit, which if it were, would account for its not having been reported in earlier texts. Nevertheless, it does look very much like an early bronze age stone circle, and it would conveniently fill a gap in the distribution map of stone circles (fig. 3.1).

I have also attempted to present reasoned arguments for the original uses of the circles; however, with little hard evidence available only a few, tentative suggestions can be made. How easy it is to speculate on their uses, especially when standing alone in the circles! One's mind can soon populate the landscape with Collingwood's 'primitive races, children of the mist', setting up their megalithic observatories with geometrical precision – quite a harmless pastime, as long as one does not confuse a past-as-can-be-known with a past-as-wished-for. Whatever the original uses of the circles, they now have, to my mind, one particular purpose – they provide very worthwhile objectives for excursions in the hills of Cumbria.

References

Abbreviations

Am. Sci.	American Scientist
Ant.	Antiquity
Arch.	Archaeologia
Arch. J.	Archaeological Journal
CBA	Council for British Archaeology
Math. Gaz.	Mathematical Gazette
Phil. Trans.	Philosophical Transactions of the Royal Society
PPS	Proceedings of the Prehistoric Society
PSAL	Proceedings of the Society of Antiquaries of London
PSAS	Proceedings of the Society of Antiquaries of Scotland
RCHM	Royal Commission for Historical Monuments
SAF	Scottish Archaeological Forum
Sci. and Arch.	Science and Archaeology
TCWAAS	Transactions of the Cumberland and Westmorland Antiquarian and Archaeological Society
TCWAAS (O.S.)	Transactions of the Cumberland and Westmorland Antiquarian and Archaeological Society (Original Series)
TLCAS	Transactions of the Lancashire and Cheshire Antiquarian Society
Ulster J. Arch.	Ulster Journal of Archaeology

References for Notes on Dating

1. G. W. Pearson, J. R. Pilcher and M. G. L. Baillie, *Radiocarbon*, 1983, vol. 25, p. 179.
2. J. Klein, J. C. Lerman, P. E. Damon and E. K. Ralph, *Radiocarbon*, 1983, vol. 24, p. 103.

References for Chapter One

1. R. H. Wood, P. Ashmead and P. A. Mellars, *North West Speleology*, 1970, vol. 1, p. 19.
2. F. Barnes and J. L. Hobbs, *TCWAAS*, 1950, vol. 50, p. 20; D. Nickson and H. McDonald, *TCWAAS*, 1955, vol. 55, p. 17.

3. J. Cherry and W. Pennington, *TCWAAS*, 1965, vol. 65, p. 66.

4. J. Cherry and P. J. Cherry, *TCWAAS*, 1973, vol. 73, p. 47.

5a. J. Cherry, *TCWAAS*, 1963, vol. 63, p. 31.

5b. J. Cherry, *TCWAAS*, 1982, vol. 82, p. 1.

6. W. Pennington, *The History of British Vegetation*, 2nd. edn., Unibooks, London, 1974.

7. J. Troels-Smith, *Danmarks Geologiske Underso/gelse*, 1960, vol. 4, p. 1.

8. W. Pennington, *Studies in the Vegetational History of the British Isles*, (eds. D. Walker and R. G. West), CUP, London, 1970, pp.41-79.

9. D. Walker, *Phil. Trans.* (B), 1966, vol. 251, p. 1.

10. F. Oldfield, *Geografiska Annaler*, 1963, vol. 45, p. 23.

11. W. Pennington, *Phil. Trans.* (B), 1964, vol. 248, p. 205.

12. R. D. Darbyshire, *Arch.*, 1874, vol. 44, p. 273.

13. E. D. Evens, L. V. Grinsell, S. Piggott and F. S. Wallis, *PPS*, 1962, vol. 28, p. 209.

14. J. M. Coles, *Archaeology by Experiment*, Hutchinson, London, 1980, p. 20.

15. J. F. S. Stone and F. S. Wallis, *PPS*, 1951, vol. 17, p. 99.

16. B. Bunch and C. I. Fell, *PPS*, 1949, vol. 15, p. 1.

17. C. I. Fell, *TCWAAS*, 1950, vol. 50, p. 1.

18. M. C. Fair, *TCWAAS*, 1943, vol. 43, p. 50.

19. J. Dobson, *TCWAAS*, 1912, vol. 12, p. 277.

20. T. H. McK. Clough, *TCWAAS*, 1973, vol. 73, p. 25.

21a. R. G. Plint, *TCWAAS*, 1962, vol. 62, p. 1.

21b. R. G. Plint, *TCWAAS*, 1978, vol. 78, p. 1.

22. T. G. Manby, *TCWAAS*, 1965, vol. 65, p. 1.

23. W. A. Cummins and C. N. Moore, *PPS*, 1973, vol. 39, p. 219.

24. E. M. Jope and J. Preston, *Ulster J. Arch.*, 1953, vol. 16, p. 31.

25. R. G. Livens, *PSAS*, 1958-9, vol. 92, p. 56.

26. P. Ashbee, *The Earthen Long Barrow in Britain*, J. M. Dent, London, 1970.

27. A. S. Hendall, *SAF*, 1970, vol. 2, p. 29.

28. W. Greenwell, *British Barrows*, Oxford, 1877, p. 389.

29. T. G. E. Powell, *TCWAAS*, 1963, vol. 63, p. 1.

30. D. Walker, *TCWAAS*, 1965, vol. 65, p. 53.

31. C. Richardson, *TCWAAS*, 1982, vol. 82, p. 7

32. I. F. Smith, *CBA Research Report*, No. 23, 1979, p. 13.

33a. T. H. McK. Clough, *TCWAAS*, 1968, vol. 68, p. 1.

33b. T. H. McK. Clough, *TCWAAS*, 1972, vol. 72, p. 44.

34. K. S. Hodgson, *TCWAAS*, 1940, vol. 40, p. 154.

35. D. Sturdy, *SAF*, 1972, vol. 4, p. 52.

36. C. I. Fell, *TCWAAS*, 1967, vol. 67, p. 17.

37. C. I. Fell, *TCWAAS*, 1940, vol. 40, p. 118.

References for Chapter Two

1. H. A. W. Burl, *The Stone Circles of the British Isles*, Yale University Press, New Haven and London, 1976.

2. F. Lynch, *SAF*, 1972, vol. 4, p. 61.
3. Ref. 1, p. 309.
4. H. A. W. Burl, *SAF*, 1972, vol. 4, p. 31.
5. J. N. G. Ritchie and A. McLaren, *SAF*, 1972, vol. 4, p. 1.
6. J. Radley, *Arch. J.*, 1966, vol. 123, p. 1.
7. A. Thom, *Megalithic Sites in Britain*, Oxford, 1967.
8. A. Thom and A. S. Thom, *Megalithic Remains in Britain and Brittany*, Oxford, 1968.
8a. op. cit. p. 22.
8b. op. cit. p. 178.
8c. op. cit. p. 179.
9. H. A. W. Burl, *Am. Sci.*, 1973, vol. 61, p. 167.
10. H. A. W. Burl, *Rings of Stone*, Frances Lincoln, London, 1979, p. 57.
11. P. Lancaster Brown, *Megaliths, Myths and Men*, Blandford, Poole, 1976.
12. D. C. Heggie, *Megalithic Science*, Thames and Hudson, London, 1981.
13. E. W. MacKie, *Science and Society in Prehistoric Britain*, Paul Elek, London, 1977.
14. T. M. Cowan, *Science*, 1970, vol. 168, p. 321.
15. I. O. Angell, *Math. Gaz.*, 1976, vol. 60, p. 189.
16. I. O. Angell, *Sci. and Arch.*, 1977, no. 19, p. 16.
17. Ref. 1, p. 74.
18. Ref. 1, p. 64.
19. Ref. 1, p. 40.
20. J. C. D. Clarke, *Economic History Review*, 1965, vol. 18, p. 1.
21. R. G. Collingwood, *TCWAAS*, 1933, vol. 33, p. 163.
22. K. S. Hodgson and K. Harper, *TCWAAS*, 1950, vol. 50, p. 30.
23. Ref. 10, p. 183.
24. A. Thom, *Megalithic Lunar Observatories*, Oxford, 1971.
25. H. A. W. Burl, *Scientific American*, 1981, vol. 245, no. 12, p. 50.
26. D. Robins, *New Scientist*, 1982, vol. 96, p. 166.
27. C. Brooker, *New Scientist*, 1983, vol. 97, p. 105.
28. M. J. O'Kelly, *New Grange: Archaeology Art and Legend*, Thames and Hudson, London, 1982, p. 82.
29. N. Lockyer, *Stonehenge and Other British Stone Monuments Astronomically Considered*, London, 1906.
30. Ref. 1, pp. 47-49.
31. Ref. 1, p. 59.
32. Ref. 1, p. 69.
33. T. G. Manby, *TCWAAS*, 1965, vol. 65, p. 1.
34. H. S. Cowper, *TCWAAS*, 1934, vol. 34, p. 91.

References for Chapter Three

1. R. G. Collingwood, *TCWAAS*, 1933, vol. 33, p. 163.
2. T. Clare, *TCWAAS*, 1975, vol. 75, p. 1.
3. T. G. E. Powell, *TCWAAS*, 1963, vol. 63, p. 1.

4. J. Dobson, *TCWAAS*, 1907, vol. 7, p. 72.

5. G. Gelderd and J. Dobson, *TCWAAS*, 1912, vol. 12, p. 262.

6. G. Gelderd, *TCWAAS*, 1922, vol. 22, p. 346.

7. F. Barnes, *TCWAAS*, 1970, vol. 70, p. 2.

8. G. Gelderd, *TCWAAS*, 1914, vol. 14, p. 466.

9. W. Bennett, *TLCAS*, 1951, vol. 62, p. 204.

10. H. S. Cowper, *TCWAAS* (O.S.), 1888, vol. IX, p. 497.

11. H. S. Cowper, *Arch.*, 1893, vol. 53, p. 419.

12. H. A. W. Burl, *Rings of Stone*, Frances Lincoln, London, 1979, p. 235.

13. C. W. Dymond, *TCWAAS*, 1902, vol. 2, p. 53.

14. C. W. Dymond, *TCWAAS* (O.S.), 1881, vol. V, p. 56.

15. H. A. W. Burl, *The Stone Circles of the British Isles*, Yale University Press, New Haven and London, 1976, p. 238.

16. J. V. S. Megaw and D. D. A. Simpson, *Introduction to British Prehistory*, Leicester University Press, 1979, p. 161.

17. J. A. Dixon and C. I. Fell, *TCWAAS*, 1948, vol. 48, p. 1.

18. J. Eccleston, *TCWAAS* (O.S.), 1874, vol. I, p. 278.

19. W. Pennington, *Studies in the Vegetational History of the British Isles*, (eds. D. Walker and R. G. West), CUP, London, 1970, pp. 41-79.

20. Ref. 15, p. 97.

21. R. Feacham, *PPS*, 1973, vol. 39, p. 332.

22. B. Williams, *PSAL*, 1856, vol. 3, p. 224.

23. C. A. Parker and W. G. Collingwood, *The Gosforth District*, Kendal, 1926, p. 80.

24. A. Thom, *Megalithic Sites in Britain*, Oxford, 1967, p. 63.

25. Ref. 23, p. 30.

26. W. Fletcher, *TCWAAS*, 1957, vol. 57, p. 1.

27. J. Cherry, *TCWAAS*, 1967, vol. 67, p. 1.

28. S. Piggott, *PSAS*, 1948, vol. 82, p. 68.

29. Ref. 24, p. 99.

30. H. Stout, *TCWAAS*, 1961, vol. 61, p. 1.

31. M. C. Fair, *TCWAAS*, 1928, vol. 28, p. 410.

32. A. Thom, *Megalithic Lunar Observatories*, Oxford, 1971, p. 71.

33. J. R. Mason and H. Valentine, *TCWAAS*, 1925, vol. 25, p. 268.

34. Ref. 15, p. 40.

35. Ref. 15, p. 93.

36. W. D. Anderson, *TCWAAS*, 1923, vol. 23, p. 29.

37. K. S. Hodgson, *TCWAAS*, 1963, vol. 63, p. 301.

38. J. Radley, *Arch. J.*, 1966, vol. 123, p. 1.

39. W. G. Collingwood, *TCWAAS*, 1926, vol. 26, p. 44.

40. W. G. Collingwood, *TCWAAS*, 1910, vol. 10, p. 342.

41. C. M. Jopling, *Arch.*, 1846, vol. 31, p. 448.

42. C. I. Fell, *TCWAAS*, 1953, vol. 53, p. 1.

43. C. I. Fell, *TCWAAS*, 1979, vol. 79, p. 143.

44. V. Jones, A. C. Bishop and A. R. Woolley, *PPS*, 1977, vol. 43, p. 287.

45. W. Hutchinson, *The History of the County of Cumberland*, Carlisle, 1794, pp. 553-4.

46. Ref. 15, p. 342.
47. Ref. 45, p. 555.
48. M. Cross and W. G. Collingwood, *TCWAAS*, 1929, vol. 29, p. 257.
49. S. Jefferson, *History of Cumberland*, Carlisle, 1842, vol. 2, p. 82.
50. Ref. 45, p. 25.
51. Ref. 49, p. 22.

References for Chapter Four

1. R. Hogg, *TCWAAS*, 1972, vol. 72, p. 1.
2. C. W. Dymond, *TCWAAS* (O.S.), 1881, vol. V, p. 50.
3. H. A. W. Burl, *The Stone Circles of the British Isles*, Yale University Press, New Haven and London, 1976.
4. B. Williams, *PSAL*, 1856, vol. 3, p. 224.
5. H. S. Cowper, *TCWAAS*, 1934, vol. 34, p. 91.
6a. J. N. G. Ritchie, *Discovery and Excavation, Scotland*, 1974, p. 79.
6b. J. N. G. Ritchie, *Arch. J.*, 1974, vol. 131, p. 1.
7. A. Thom, *Megalithic Sites in Britain*, Oxford, 1967, p. 145.
8. Ref. 7, p. 150.
9. Ref. 7, p. 151.
10. W. D. Anderson, *TCWAAS*, 1923, vol. 23, p. 109.
11. W. D. Anderson, *TCWAAS*, 1915, vol. 15, p. 99.
12. W. Stukeley, *Iterarium Curiosum*, vol. 2, London, 1776, p. 48.
13. Ref. 7, p. 139.
14. Ref. 3, p. 89.
15. K. S. Hodgson, *TCWAAS*, 1935, vol. 35, p. 77.
16. Ref. 12, p. 47.
17. W. Camden, *Britannia*, Gough's Edition of 1806, vol. 3, p. 444.
18. Ref. 12, p. 47.
19. O. G. S. Crawford, *Ant.*, 1934, vol. 8, p. 328.
20. W. G. Collingwood, *TCWAAS*, 1913, vol. 13, p. 406.
21. W. G. Collingwood, *The Lake Counties*, J. M. Dent & Sons, London, 1949, p. 258.
22. W. Thornley, *TCWAAS*, 1902, vol. 2, p. 380.
23. Ref. 7, p. 144.
24. Ref. 7, p. 109
25. W. G. Collingwood, *TCWAAS*, 1901, vol. 1, p. 295.
26. K. S. Hodgson, *TCWAAS*, 1952, vol. 52, p. 1.
27. G. G. S. Richardson and C. I. Fell, *TCWAAS*, 1975, vol. 75, p. 17.
28. K. S. Hodgson, *TCWAAS*, 1935, vol. 35, p. 77.
29. K. S. Hodgson and K. Harper, *TCWAAS*, 1950, vol. 50, p. 30.
30. C. B. Burgess, *The Age of Stonehenge*, J. M. Dent & Sons, London, 1980, pp. 68 and 186.
31. Ref. 30, p. 106.
32. J. Robinson and R. S. Ferguson, *TCWAAS* (O.S.), 1881, vol. V, p. 76.

33. Ref. 7, p. 69.
34. M. W. Taylor, *TCWAAS* (O.S.), 1886, vol. VIII, p. 323.
35. J. E. Spence, *TCWAAS*, 1934, vol. 34, p. 45.
36. RCHM (Westmorland), 1936, p. 26.
37. E. Noble, *TCWAAS*, 1907, vol. 7, p. 211.
38. J. Simpson, *Arch. J.*, 1861, vol. 18, p. 25.
39. W. Greenwell, *TCWAAS* (O.S.), 1874, vol. I, p. 19.
40. W. Greenwell, *British Barrows*, Oxford, 1877, p. 400.
41. J. Simpson, *PSAS* (1st series), 1863, vol. IV, p. 443.
42. A. Wainwright, *The Far Eastern Fells*, Kendal, 1957.
43. Ref. 36, p. 39.
44. Ref. 36, p. 40.
45. Ref. 3, p. 59.
46. T. Pennant, *A Tour in Scotland*, 3rd edn., Warrington, 1774, p. 258.
47. Ref. 36, p. 206.
48. T. Clare, *TCWAAS*, 1978, vol. 78, p. 5.
49. J. Nicolson and R. Burn, *The History and Antiquities of the Counties of Westmorland and Cumberland*, London, 1777, p. 477.
50. G. Hall, *Gentleman's Magazine*, 1824, p. 3.
51. C. W. Dymond, *TCWAAS* (O.S.), 1880, vol. IV, p. 537.
52. Ref. 7, p. 72.
53. G. F. Weston, *TCWAAS* (O.S.), 1876, vol. II, p. 205.
54. R. G. Collingwood, *TCWAAS*, 1933, vol. 33, p. 201.
55. Ref. 3, p. 271.
56. C. I. Fell, *TCWAAS*, 1964, vol. 64, p. 408.
57. R. S. Ferguson, *TCWAAS* (O.S.), 1883, vol. VI, p. 183.
58. H. S. Cowper, *TCWAAS*, 1934, vol. 34, p. 91.
59. C. W. Dymond, *TCWAAS* (O.S.), 1891, vol. XI, p. 187.
60. Ref. 46, p. 256.
61. Ref. 12, p. 44.
62. Harkness, *TCWAAS* (O.S.), 1876, vol. III, p. xvi.
63. G. Bersu, *TCWAAS*, 1940, vol. 40, p. 169.
64. R. G. Collingwood, *TCWAAS*, 1938, vol. 38, p. 1.
65. Ref. 12, p. 43.
66. Ref. 49, p. 495.
67. G. Rome-Hall, *TCWAAS* (O.S.), 1883, vol. VI, p. 468.
68. T. H. B. Graham, *TCWAAS*, 1967, vol. 67, p. 7.
69. R. S. Ferguson, *Victoria County History, Cumberland*, 1901, vol. 1, p. 245.
70. K. S. Hodgson, *TCWAAS*, 1935, vol. 35, p. 78.
71. W. Hutchinson, *The History of the County of Cumberland*, Carlisle, 1774, p. 175.
72. Ref. 3, p. 61.
73. J. E. Spence, *TCWAAS*, 1935, vol. 35, p. 69.
74. Ref. 3, p. 342.
75. Ref. 46, p. 257.
76. Ref. 49, p. 323.

77. W. Whellan, *The History and Topography of the Counties of Cumberland and Westmorland*, Pontefract, 1860, p. 161.
78. H. Rooke, *Arch.*, 1792, vol. 10, p. 105.
79. W. G. Collingwood, *TCWAAS*, 1923, vol. 23, p. 256.
80. Ref. 3, p. 343.
81. Ref. 49, p. 529.
82. J. Hodgson, *A Topographical and Historical Description of the County of Westmoreland*, 1820, p. 223.

Reference for Postscript

1. R. G. Flint, *TCWAAS*, 1960, vol. 60, p. 201.

Index

Entries in bold denote the main discussion for stone circle sites only; entries in italics denote references to figures.